WITNESS

KEEP YOUR HAND ON THE PLOW

JANETTE JONES

ISBN: 979-8-89031-925-8 (sc)
ISBN: 979-8-89031-926-5 (hc)
ISBN: 979-8-89031-927-2 (e)

Because of the dynamic nature of the Internet, any web addresses or links contained in this book may have changed since publication and may no longer be valid. The views expressed in this work are solely those of the author and do not necessarily reflect the views of the publisher, and the publisher hereby disclaims any responsibility for them.

THE EWINGS
PUBLISHING

One Galleria Blvd., Suite 1900, Metairie, LA 70001
(504) 702-6708

CONTENTS

ABOUT THE AUTHOR

Janette is an ordained elder in the African Methodist Episcopal Church and currently serves as an associate minister at Allen Chapel AME Church located in South Omaha.

As an accomplished playwright, director and producer in 2002 Janette's first stage production titled *Sistah Girl,* came to fruition and received rave reviews. *Sistah Girl Revisited* debuted in 2005. As a tribute to a beloved deceased cast member Sistah *Girl Now & Again* was presented in 2008 at the Witherspoon Concert Hall. As an author, *Cloudy Witness: Blessedly Assured,* published in 2012 and its sequel *Finding a Happy Medium: Let the Redeemed Say So,* published in 2018, wasn't long in coming to fruition..

Janette was a featured personality in the Emmy Award winning 2009 documentary, *'An Inaugural Ride to Freedom: The Legacy of a People, a Movement, and a Mission,'* an Omowale Akintunde film. The documentary was a depiction of a cross country bus trip made by college students, and members of the Omaha community to the inauguration of President Barak Obama. She was later cast in Akintunde's 2010 film *'Wigger.'*

Make My Day Floral Creations is a home-based business Janette started over twenty some years ago which is a make up of event planning, fashion show production and floral designing. Janette's floral designs have been commissioned from clients as far away as Chicago, Arizona, Texas, California, as well as Georgia.

The native North Carolinian couple, Janette and her husband Jerry, traveled extensively as a prior military family to such faraway places as Germany, France, Belgium, Austria, the Bahamas, and the United Kingdom.

The Joneses are the proud parents and grandparents of three adult children and three grandchildren.

REV. BENJAMIN R. FINNELL'S

FOREWORD

It has been a decade since Rev. Janette Jones set in motion a masterpiece consisting of encounters with the supernatural by quite ordinary folk that we all can identify with. Rereading the book I am struck with the freshness and appeal it still possesses. When one begins to read *Cloudy Witness* we are introduced to each character and one wonders who does he/she remind me of. Read on and each character begins to leap off the page into our own psyche and as the drama unfolds one must remind oneself that this is Christian fiction and yet ask could it be? Is this real? The language is the speech of everyday people, full of grit and spirit. The reading is easy and flows seamlessly from one scene to another. Nothing is left out but to get all the answers one must keep on reading. If you have not had an encounter like the one that is described in the following pages as our ancestors used to say," just keep on living". OH, by the way, did I say that this is fiction?

Cloudy Witness is a timeless piece of Christian fiction that should be read by all. You will not be disappointed; you will want to hurry to see what happens next as well as what will be the outcome. Afterwards reading the sequel, *Finding a Happy Medium* is a must.

Enjoy, and may God bless you and keep you is our prayer.

Rev. Benjamin R. Finnell

REV. DR. SAMUEL LOFTON, III

FOREWORD

There is an art of storytelling and not everyone should step forward. Thankfully, that's not the case for Janette Jones because she has done it again!

She continues to demonstrate the importance of spiritual imagination in life's journey while remaining true to one's interpretation of Scripture. Janette Jones is no stranger to capturing our curiosity about things seen and unseen. Her previous work, *Cloudy Witness: Blessed Assured,* invited her readers to imagine the possibilities and embrace the mysteries spoken in God's Word. It was what avid readers call a "page turner". When you finally put the book down, it was plain to see that Janette is a storyteller of the utmost degree and a person firmly grounded in her faith with a gift for removing the veil to the small glimpses of heaven crafted in the mind of a willing servant.

John Walsh, Founder of The Christian Storytelling Network, informs that "People don't make decisions based on facts they hear or even know. They make decisions based on what they have experienced." If you take this journey with Janette Jones and the characters of *Cloudy Witness:* Keep Your Hand on the Plow... Anniversary Edition, you will experience a story that tugs at your heart strings, tickles your funny bone, and causes you to scratch your head; more importantly, you will find yourself thanking yourself for looking beyond the limits of one-dimensional thinking into one where you can fathom mysteries revealed and witnessed by those willing to only imagine.

Rev. Dr. Samuel Lofton III, D. Min.
Men's Ministry Director, Victory Apostolic Church

PREFACE

It has taken nearly a year to write this book. But I feel I was being prepared for it for quite some time. Finally, after "giving myself away" for many late hours until this awe-inspiring work of Christian fiction came into existence.

Cloudy Witness: Blessedly Assured derived from a 'night vision,' whereby Hebrews 12:1 was made manifest to the author.

Therefore, since we are surrounded by such a great cloud of witnesses, let us put off everything that so easily entangles, and let us run with patience this race marked out for us. NIV

If given the opportunity to interact with the likes of 'the first family' Adam and Eve what do you suppose your reaction would be?

Well, for seven unsuspecting friends whose day-to-day activities are intercepted by the paranormal of the biblical-kind it was life-changing.

Etta Mae and Donnie Smith, Tonika and Josh Gibbons, Delilah and Damien Whitman, along with Stephanie Willis, all face life altering encounters. Two of which even hold audience with a lone covert figure clothe in all-white.

Along with the saints of old, we're also encompassed about by evil entities as well. In this moving drama, anticipate displays of anger, defiant attitudes, as well as rejoicing, as the seven fictive characters interact with the likes of Jezebel, and the wife of Potiphar.

This literary work is comprised of fictional characters taken from *Sistah Girl* series of stage productions written, produced and directed by the author.

Sistah Girl, an epic adaptation of the lives of twelve biblical women impacting the lives of fictive modern- day personalities. Each time receiving rave reviews from local audiences.

After reading *Cloudy Witness,* the reader may be found conducting an in-depth interrogation of their own spiritual commitment.

As a disclaimer, this work of fiction is not intended to diminish the validity of the Holy Bible from which references were taken. Neither was it written in a judgmental viewpoint of one's life choices. For we rejoice in knowing our Lord and Savior, Jesus Christ does not judge us before we obtain His grace and mercy.

Soul searching questions that may arise are: Would I be able to cope with the life shattering crisis if I found myself in the same situation? Do I have the blessed assurance I've ran with patience this earthly race? Am I; *"Looking unto Jesus, the author and finisher of my faith?"* Heb. 12:2aNIV

These and perhaps other questions may only be answered through the heart cry of King David:

"Search me, O God, and know my heart; test me and know my anxious thoughts." Psalm 139 NIV

CHAPTER

One

I n a state of discomposure, the mocha complexioned 5'10"
thirty-nine-year-old's heavy locks, usually pulled back in a bouncing
elongated ponytail couldn't help fully knowing her five-year marriage was
now over.

Tonika Gibbons the only child of a black army sergeant father and
German national mother, walked out of her clothe strewn bedroom
absentmindedly twirling 'bedhead' tousled hair through long tapered
fingers. She hadn't slept well during the night, The Floyd family called
Fayetteburg, North Carolina their permanent home at the end of her
father's tour of duty in Germany. Tonika later enrolled and attended
college in Fayetteburg. However, stationary life such as college was not
the adventure seeker's cup of tea. With discontentment soon becoming her
nemesis, later dropping out during her sophomore year.

Soon afterwards, in a year's time, Tonika met and married Jamal
Tulufano, an American Samoan. Later, after suffering a tragic loss, Jamal
walked away from the marriage, leaving behind a forlorn Tonika and
a young son. The adorable couple soon found themselves relocating to
New Jersey for the sake of Jamal's construction job. Unfortunately, that
marriage had only lasted for four years.

With a tousled-haired son resulting from a short union of four years,
and no longer viewing the world through rose colored glasses, the newly

divorcee could only then begin meeting life head on by taking it one day at a time.

Then one day a tall, handsome, aspiring entrepreneur by the name of Josh Gibbons walked into her life

Thinking back on it, if the sly smile that had first captivated her attention was any indication of where she now stands the nearest exit door would've been a true Godsend.

"Note to self…from here on out Tonika gir-rrl! Keep your guard up at all time!" The forlorn housewife shouted in air.

Josh's number one priority in life was to become the owner of a lucrative sportswear/shoe business.

Before he and Tonika married, he'd tried his hand at bringing his dream to fruition, only to fall prey to several get-rich-quick schemes.

But the day JG's Trendy Duds opened its doors the man's confidence was boosted to new heights. The hip-hop clothing store had been located on the first floor of the Shady Brooks Mal. Which in the beginning had been a huge success.

But, as fate would have it, this too had proven unprofitable as time went on. The dated inventory hadn't been able to keep pace with the trendy, hip hop styles of teenage mind-sets.

After he'd fallen behind on his monthly rental fee and other business expenditures the store had folded.

The adamant dreamer, equipped with strong determination, had vowed he would someday become the successful entrepreneur he longed to be.

This morning, as time would have it, the scorned inamorata found herself on the short end of yet another marital relationship gone sour.

She grabbed a tissue from the marble kitchen counter and forcibly blew her high-bridged nose that had been rubbed raw after a night of weeping.

The scene that had led to Josh storming out of the house with his suitcase that morning resurfaced in her thoughts.

After the biggest argument of their marriage, she had gotten up, and had locked the bedroom door when she'd heard his car pull into the driveway, extremely late. Josh had slept on the couch.

The incident that had led up to all the drama had all started when he'd returned home from work. Josh hadn't noticed the folded paper that had fallen from his shirt pocket while hastily discarding his clothing.

Tonika had sauntered into the bedroom hoping to set their date-night in motion.

"Hey, babe, I thought we might go out to a movie after dinner; what 'a ya' say?"

The folded sheet of paper lying on the floor caught her eye. As she'd bent to pick it up, a series of uncontrollable sneezing ensued brought on by a whiff of unfamiliar perfume. She had unfolded the paper and feverishly scanned the contents.

"What the hell?" She blurted hardly believing her eyes.

"O, my God!"

The sound of the running water coming from the shower could be heard through the bathroom door.

The scorned woman had burst into the steamy bathroom, and in a quick swoop had angrily thrown back the shower curtain.

"What-da? Hey! Tonika what are you doing?" Josh had exclaimed.

"What in the hell is this?" She had demanded, holding the crunched paper in her fist.

Josh had grabbed for a towel before stepping out of the shower.

Tonika had begun to read the contents of the note with wrathful fervor.

"I'm still basking in the glow of our love from our night together. I can't wait to be with you again. Hurry back, lover boy."

He had reached for the critical evidence she was holding, but she'd backed out of his reach. Tonika had thrown the crumpled paper in his face and had stormed out of the bathroom.

The realization of knowing he had been caught red handed took a while to sink in. Finally, he'd concluded it was pointless to offer any form of explanation.

Josh had shrugged his shoulders in defeat. He had infact, actually found the disclosure of the matter a blessed relief. To the point he had even contemplated putting an end to their marital facade for some time.

Admittedly, the endless amount of time his wife spent with their neighbor, a devout Christian from across the street, had left him with a void feeling.

He had thought of how increasingly disheartened he had become lately in their intimate relationship but hadn't known how to approach the matter of separating.

He hadn't known exactly when the luster had left, but only knew he no longer felt the way he once had.

There had been a time when the daring lioness' uninhibited prowess in the boudoir had left little room for complaint for the virile 'stud muffin.'

"Well... as fate would have it, no better time than now." The exposed cheater had thought.

He couldn't help but reflect on how he had reached this point in his life.

After the loss of his last business venture, his only other option had been to return to the ineffective workforce.

The housing market had taken a downward turn, which left Tonika's contribution to their household finances very limited.

He had soon gained employment at the Enterprise Telemarketing Corporation (ETC) as a sales rep and had quickly become a top salesman.

Karla Jordan, an upwardly mobile senior accountant for the firm, three years Josh's junior, had unexpectedly captured his interest.

A picture of beauty with a drop- dead figure, and a head of highlighted bouncy curls had sashayed into the company's cafeteria one day.

The above-the-knee skin tight periwinkle pencil skirt had held Josh mesmerized. A glimpse of ample breast could be seen through the peek-a-boo hole in the multi colored, form fitting top.

The grilled chicken breast sandwich had lain untouched as his eyes had followed her every move. Their eyes had briefly met.

"Man, look at that! Who does *that* belong to?" The gawking man had said to Steven Cox, a co-worker who shared the adjacent cubicle.

Steven's eyes had followed the salivating man's gaze but had quickly dropped and had issued a strict warning.

"Stay away from that, dude. You don't want to mess with her. That's 'Miss Fire Starter.' Believe me when I tell you. The woman's bad news."

"Oh! Is that right? So, she's a fire starter, huh?" The foreboding co-worker's cautious warning had only heightened the enamored suitor's interest more.

"In other words, don't ignite the kindling if you can't extinguish the flames. You catch my drift?" Then Steven had quickly added. "Especially, with you being a married man and all!"

Josh had stopped listening after hearing "fire starter." He felt as if he just had to get to know the beguiling temptress better.

His feet had propelled him to rise, leaving Steven with a startled look. Josh made his way out of the cafeteria and had hesitantly approached Karla on the veranda.

"Excuse me, but i-is this seat taken?" He'd timidly asked.

Karla ran her eyes up and down the length of the magnificent specimen that stood before her.

She liked what she saw. Sizing up her prey, she'd quickly made a mental note of the platinum wedding band on his left finger and had smiled mischievously. The wedding band made no difference to the well-known "home wrecker."

"It will be... once you sit down, 'First Sergeant.'" She'd said, smiling seductively.

The smooth skinned six-foot hunk standing timidly before her reminded Karla of a favorite television commercial that had once aired.

A ranked army officer was always greeted by his troops with a "Good morning, First Sergeant."

Karla and her rowdy girlfriends had forever been infatuated with the handsome male figure featured in the popular commercial.

To that point, she was often found sizing all dating prospects to his likeness. Needless to say, Josh had been warmly received, and the 'match' had been lit.

Josh brought his thoughts back to the moment at hand. The six-month tryst with Karla had now been exposed, thanks to a little white note. It had never been his intention for his wife to find out about his extra marital affair, especially in such a way.

His mind had gone back to the initial conversation he'd had with the co-worker. "Fire Starter" had been what he'd called her. That she was and then some!"

An all-knowing smile had spread across his face at the recollection of their ravaged lovemaking. Karla had slipped the note into his shirt pocket as she came up behind his chair.

She had allowed his head to be cupped in her breasts before stealing away, with a knowing grin on her face. The unexpected gesture had caused the phone to fall from the surprised lover's hand.

After retrieving the fallen receiver, he had hastily offered the unfortunate customer at the other end a hurried apology. The affectionate display had not been lost on Steven, or any of the other co-workers.

The love-struck buck had meant to destroy the note after reading it, but had been distracted by Steven, who had leaned over from his cubicle and accosted him.

"I saw that… man just be careful, please!" He had cautiously said. "Don't say I didn't warn you."

"That bloke is surely asking for trouble."

Steven had sternly said to Stephanie Willis, his co-worker seated across from him.

"Yes, he sure is, because I know his wife!"

Stephanie had eagerly awaited an opportunity to share the juicy gossip with her lunch buddies.

"What to do, what to do…" Josh had thought to himself as he dried the beads of water from his torso. The only thing to do now he'd concluded was to go out and confront the angry 'she bear.'

The thought of the pending confrontation had caused drops of sweat to trickle down his already wet brow.

In the bedroom, Tonika had shivered in the evening coolness as she sat at the end of the bed. The billowing chiffon curtains that brushed against her leg had caused her to suddenly flinch.

Uncontrollable tears had run down the betrayed woman's face as she sat there.

Finally, what seemed to her like an eternity, the door to the bathroom had hesitantly opened. Josh had stood there wrapped in a towel.

At the sound of the opening door, the instinct of attack had overtaken the 'screaming banshee.' She had sprang from the bed with arms flailing yelling at the top of her lungs.

"Who is she? You cheating bastard! How could you do this to me?"

"Stop it Toni! Now, I'm warning you, you don't want to do this."

Josh had tried to catch a hold of the flailing arms and had drastically tried to deflect the wild blows.

Smaaack!

The sound had echoed. She had swung her fist once again and had slapped the traitor with an open hand across his wet face.

His face had burned from the sting of the blow. He had pushed the out-of-control dynamo down onto the bed, but she'd jumped up once again.

"Damn it, woman, stop it, I said!"

He had somehow managed to turn her taut body around with her arms crisscrossed and had held on tightly.

The room had been filled with both their heavy breathing. She had frantically squirmed while trying to loosen the tight grip he had on her wrists.

"Let me go you traitor, get off me!" She had muttered through clenched teeth, steadily squirming.

"I mean it; let me go and don't you ever touch me again!"

"Okay, okay.... I'm going to let go of you, but damn it, don't start swinging at me again." Josh said, hesitantly loosening his grip. "Now I mean it Toni!"

He had given her a slight shove and had stepped back, which had caused her to lose her balance. She had corrected her footing and had rubbed her wrist to regain circulation.

"Well... I'm listening." She had said to Josh in between deep, wrenching breaths.

The 'muddled betrayer of his marriage vows' had sat down in the Parson's chair with his lowered head grasped in his hands. She had remained standing with arms defiantly folded.

"Tonika … now look." Josh had released a long sigh. "I'm sorry…okay? But it's just not working out, and it hasn't been for a very long time." He looked forlornly at his sobbing wife. "And you know for yourself it hasn't; so why fool ourselves?"

The broken-hearted woman hadn't bothered to wipe away the hot, salty tears that had rolled down her face.

"I've been meaning to tell you, but I just couldn't seem to find the right time." Josh had gone on to say. "But… now that you know; you know. It's just that simple."

The fuming woman had shifted her weight from one foot to the other. It had been all she could do not to land another well deserving blow.

"If it makes you feel any better, I'll be out of your hair by tomorrow morning. Just give me time to gather all my things."

He had gone over to his chest of drawers. The last remark, however, hadn't sat well with the discarded home-maker. She had stormed over behind him and had forcibly spun the culpable traitor around.

"Oh! So, it's just that simple, huh? And just how're you going to fix your *damn* mouth to say, it's just that simple?

There's nothing simple about any of this bull! As a matter of fact, why don't you just get all your punk trash, and get out right now!" She had stomped her foot.

"Just get the hell out!"

Tonika had brushed the startled man aside and had grabbed neatly folded clothes from a drawer, and had thrown them all into the hallway.

"I'm sick of you, and I don't want to see your ugly face around here ever again!"

"Damn it girl! You didn't have to do all that." Josh had said, as he bent to retrieve his favorite football jersey and blue jeans.

"I said I was sorry, now back off!"

"You're sorry? Is that all you can fix your damn mouth to say to me; you're sorry?"

It felt as if the wind had been knocked out of her, she had sat down on the bed and had begun to weep once again.

Josh had merely shrugged his shoulders and had returned to the task of locating the articles of clothing.

After dressing, he had grabbed his car keys and had left the room, leaving behind a duped victim.

"I'm coming back in the morning to get my things." He had yelled from the kitchen.

The exhausted, deserted woman had fallen back on the bed and had sobbed a river of tears.

Bewildered, she'd wondered just how so much water could come from one person. She had rolled over and had beaten the pillow with her fist.

"Damn you woman, whoever you are; damn, damn, damn you!"

Tonika reasoned she would go over to her friend's house tomorrow and have a good cry on her shoulder.

Maybe she could help make sense of everything. She had cried herself to sleep.

The next morning, she lay motionless while sunlight flowed into the room. Tonika reflected on the previous day's occurrence. All she knew was that she had given their marriage her full devotion for the past five years.

She thought of how she'd noticed a change come over him. How he'd become abstractedly distant. There'd been the times he'd arrived home late from work without bothering to offer any explanation.

She remembered how he'd once copped an attitude with her about the amount of time she'd spent in Bible study and church with Etta Mae, so she'd chalked it up to that.

No doubt, she had grown spiritually under her friend's tutelage. Her parents' free-will attitude had allowed her to choose whether or not she'd wanted to practice any form of religion while growing up. It had also been the same for Josh.

Tonika was overcome with a sense of foreboding. Just the thought of becoming a single parent once again was frightening. Her mind retreated to her first marriage, and how she and Jamal had greatly anticipated having a brood of kids.

They'd wanted at least two boys and two girls. After trying for some time, the jubilant couple had learned Ashad, their first child, would soon become 'big brother' to a little sister.

Her name was to have been Adrika. The two children would've been a year apart in age. However, the couple's joy had been short lived when she had suffered a miscarriage in the third trimester. This was due largely to a sub mucosal fibroid tumor that had grown along with the baby inside her uterus.

Tonika had awakened one night from a fitful sleep to find her bed linen soaked with blood. Jamal had rushed her to the emergency room. There, they'd soon learned the placenta had separated from her uterine wall. Their infant daughter had succumbed in the womb from the lack of oxygen.

She had received two blood transfusions after having become chronically anemic. The AIDs scare had been in full bloom at the time, so the thought of having to receive a stranger's blood had left her with frayed nerves. She'd watched with dismay as the red life-giving substance had crept slowly down the tube and into her arm.

After the little coffin was interred, life in their household had gone downhill from there. Jamal had suffered with a bout of depression and never recovered from their loss. Tonika had often wondered if he had somehow blamed her. Then one day, unexpectedly, he had just up and left.

Jamal's departure had left her in a terrible state of mind as well, along with a financial bind. Work as a real estate agent had proven to be an unprofitable venture in the days of economic recession. No one was buying, and no one was selling.

But, through it all, she had made it, even as her savings had slowly dwindled. Thank God, for her sweet, kind neighbors. She would be forever grateful to Donnie and Etta Mae Smith. They'd watched two-year old Ashad nearly every other night for years while she had moonlighted as a hostess at a swank restaurant.

She had met Josh at that same restaurant. He'd been everything she'd been looking for in a marriage partner. Ashad finally had a father figure in his life.

"Well…here goes, there's no use hoping the cheat will stick around after this."

The void his infidelity had caused in their relationship was much too vast to mend.

"No use in my hanging on to wishful thinking."

Tonika resolved that she would allow the cheater to return and gather his belongings. It was mostly clothes anyways. Thankfully, her home had already been established when they'd married.

Josh had come into the relationship with nothing more than his treasured classic red Trans Am. Yet, he had shared his limited finances unselfishly. All in all, he had more than adequately provided for their family.

CHAPTER

Two

....

"Angels! O, my God! The sky is full of angels! A-and there's a figure sitting on a throne! My Lord! Is that -"

The vision vanished just as quickly as it manifested. Sleep filled eyes flew open.

"No-oo! It mustn't end; it was too beautiful!"

The fifty-something registered nurse with skin the tone of pure cocoa, commanded her ample body to lie still, trying to comprehend it all.

"I just had a 'night vision!' I was just blessed with a supernatural glimpse of Heaven. My, my, what was that all about?"

Etta Mae Smith's mind was bombarded with all sorts of possibilities.

"Wait!" A keen thought had suddenly registered.

She recalled reading how a prophet had once saw 'ten foot' angels come through his church walls. Heck, according to that prophet, even Jesus had made an appearance, and had walked the church isles.

"Maybe, there'll be an 'open heaven' phenomenon. Yes, something like that may come to pass today."

"Wouldn't that be wonderful? Shucks you never know. One thing for sure, man can't put our God in a box.

To say He speaks this way, or He does things that way is questionable, because 'the Almighty' does what He desires to do. When He desires to do it. And how He desires to do it! Why? Simply, be-e-cau-ze He's Sovereign!"

A hint of daylight eluded the corners of the 'light blocker' shades. Groggy eyes focused on the clothing scattered around the room.

The disheveled appearance of the room was the result of her husband's frantic search for an article of clothing he somehow convinced himself he desperately needs.

"Darn, the sun is up already. Am I ready to meet this day?"

"One thing for sure, with 'DST' your day begins bright and early, whether you're ready to face it or not. Where does man get off messing with time anyway?"

In a measure of unraveling her twisted night gown from around her waist the now fully awakened matron allowed a huge sigh to escape her lips while feeling the space next to her. The space was empty. She then rose on one elbow and looked inquiringly at the vacant spot.

"What the heck?"

She said while making quick work of tucking an annoying wisp of hair underneath the silk night cap.

"Where's that man?" Looking around. "What time is it anyway?"

Etta Mae glanced at the clock on the nightstand and threw both legs over the side of the bed.

It's only six o'clock in the morning. She thought. "*Humph*, now I know that fool can't already be on that darn golf course."

She, of course, was referring to her husband of thirty-eight years, Donnie Leroy Smith.

"I hate to say it, but the love that man has for that blessed game borders on obsession."

"Shucks, come to think of it, football widows don't have anything on me."

An annoying ache in her left shoulder was causing her considerable discomfort.

She rotated the shoulder in a circular motion hoping to relieve the stiffness.

The dull ache resulted from a shoulder impingement brought on by a bursitis flare up.

The flare-ups seemed to be occurring more frequently. Although, sometimes, just lying on her right side would offer a bit of welcomed relief.

There had been a time she welcomed having the full range of the bed to herself. But not this morning. Pain or no pain, she needed to share her experience.

Although, it wasn't as if the old man could offer any semblance of an interpretation. That's just not in him. She thought. But heck, just being able to share it with him would have made the dream… correction vision more surreal.

"Hey babe…" Donnie had entered the bedroom scratching his head.

Her husband's sudden appearance had caused her to jump and clutch at her chest.

"Donnie! You scared the heck out of me!"

"Sorry hon! I didn't mean to." He was startled by her sudden reaction.

"I thought you were on the ninth hole by now."

"Now, why would you think that? You know I don't go to the clubhouse 'til eight o'clock."

"Oh, I don't know what to think anymore!" Etta Mae said, yawning and rubbing her eyes. "I didn't realize it was so darn early."

"It's a mystery to me how you're even awake, especially after last night. What's going on with you anyways?"

Donnie not honestly expecting an answer went on to inquire about a particular article of clothing.

"Have you seen my gray paisley golf shirt?"

He frantically began sorting through a pile of clothing lying in a chair.

"I know I left it here… I've looked everywhere for it."

"You and that darn shirt." Etta Mae blurted, not actually admitting to having seen it.

"I sure hope you haven't put it in the wash, you know I never wash my 'good luck charm' whenever I'm in a big tournament."

"The whole county knows you never…" His befuddled soulmate added. We know that's a big no, no!"

Choosing to ignore his wife's callous sarcasm Donnie continued with his frantic search.

"All the 'karma' might be washed out of it." Donnie added.

"Honey, I was going to tell you about this vision I had."

Etta Mae's mind had long since dismissed the whereabouts of the missing shirt. Returning her thoughts once again to her unsettling dream instead.

"I'm glad you got some sleep, because no one else did… mainly me."

Stopping in his tracks the now perplexed husband watched his wife with concern.

"Who could sleep with you mumbling and moving about?"

"I was? …and you say I was mumbling too?"

"Yes, and you were talking some mumbo jumbo. So, I figured I'd might as well get up and get a head start on my day.

That is… if I can find my darn shirt! Etta Mae… honey, you sure you haven't seen it?"

His wife's curiosity was now piqued to new heights regarding her fitful sleep. She stared balefully at the distracted man yanking hard on his arm.

"I was mumbling. What was I mumbling, do you remember?"

But Donnie's distracted with his own concerns.

"Let's see I pulled my shirt off in the dining room yesterday."

"Honey, are you listening? Did you hear what I just asked you?"

"I'm sorry, but what did you just ask me?" Now turning his attention to his wife again.

"Oh, yeah, when you weren't snoring, you were mumbling something like; "Yes, Lord, yes, Lord."

"What're you talking about? …I don't snore!"

"No! You don't snore! Calling hogs is more like it. And it was loud!"

"Don-nie, stop it!" Etta Mae defiantly repeated. I said I don't snore!" "Now you, on the other hand…"

"Well, call it what you want! But I could've sworn we had a concert going on up in here." Donnie snickered. "And you were out snoring me! Shuck It even woke me up!"

He continued to replay his wife's bed-time drama.

"And then you started singing, and I thought you were going to leap right off the bed."

15

"Shut up! Donnie you lieing!" Etta Mae playfully exclaimed. "And I was singing too?"

She couldn't help but laugh and reached out to take her honey's hand.

"Honey... *what* was I singing? Go on, sing it for me."

Donnie wondering whether his wife was losing it resolved in the end to humor her.

"Ah-h, now Ett-aa." He reluctantly said. "Okay, darn! I shouldn't even have brought it up."

"Oh, would 'ya do it already!"

"Okay, okay!"

Donnie prepared to mimic his wife's rendition in a voice that was none too pleasing to the ears.

"I believe it went something like....

"K-Keep your hand on-n the pl-ow-w!" And ho-old on!

He sang in his baritone voice. They both couldn't help but laugh.

"Then you started waving your arms and wiggling your feet."

Donnie's demonstration was a bit over exaggerated, to say the least. His wife thought.

"About that time, I'd had enough. So, I jumped up and was going into the other room, but I remembered an uninvited guest was in there. So, I went into the office and laid on the futon."

"We-ell, 'scuse me! Didn't mean to disturb that precious sleep of yours." She sarcastically offered.

"But honey! In my dream, my hands were on a plow! And it was turning over rich and fertile soil!" The jubilant woman recalled.

"You; plowing?" Now that had to be a dream."

"Oh quit it!" She said playfully. "Oh, and my sister will be with us for a couple of days. I hope you don't mind.

"Na, I don't mind. Why would I mind?"

"Oh, I knew you didn't, but just out of respect. Thank you."

"Just listen to this!" The over exuberant dreamer casting a meaningful eye at the love of soul said.

"Okay, okay, I'm all ears Etta." Donnie said. Let's hear about this so-called dream of yours."

"Good ... She said giving her wonderful, understanding husband a love pat.

"Now like I said, I was plowing a field, but please don't ask me what field, 'cause I couldn't tell you.

But get this... there wasn't a horse, or an ox pulling the plow. Just me walking behind a plow."

"Now, how're you gon'na just up and plow a field without a horse or an ox to pull the plow?" Donnie countered.

Seeing the staunch look directed his direction Donnie soon quieted the unwanted questioning.

"Sorry, my bad. Please, do continue." He motioned.

"Well...as I plowed, the hard earth was breaking up, and that hard soil turned into this rich black dirt; you know, like rich potting soil." Etta Mae exclaimed. "It was the blackest dirt I'd ever seen."

"Now...you said blacker than potting soil?" Donnie interjected once again. "Now that's some black, and some rich soil."

"Honey! Do you want to hear this or not?"

"Okay, okay. Again! I'm sorry. Just trying to picture you behind a plow. Donnie amusingly added "Now that had to be-

"Donnie Le-Roy Smith, I swear, if you don't!"

"Okay Etta! But finish already! My Lord!

"Alright, alright, already! Donnie throwing up his hands in surrender giving a now clearly agitated storyteller his full attention. "Geez!"

Etta then continued telling her tale. "But I do remember feeling as if I was floating."

"Hey...that reminds me".

Spreading her arms in demonstration Etta Mae began singing the words to a song she'd once forgotten.

"When my ways get dark as night. Keep your hands on-n that plow, ho-old on. Had no one to go their bail. Keep your hands on-nn that plow. A-nnd ho-old on!"

Surprisingly, throwing his head back, and stomping his feet Donnie finishes the song.

"Hold on-n! Ho-old on. Keep your hand on-n that plow, and just ho-old on."

They both laughed.

"And that dear Etta is from my girl Mahalia! Actually, it's from scripture." Donnie pleasingly offered. "Yeah, yeah! Luke 9:62 in fact."

Oh…scared of you." Etta said amazed at her husband's scripture savy. "Quoting scripture and all."

"Will wonders never cease you ask?" Donnie jokingly continues. "Jesus said in Luke 9: *No one who puts their hand to the plow and looks back is fit for the service in the kingdom of God.*"

"Amen and amen!" Donnie said doing a mock bow.

Etta Mae couldn't help but be impressed. Given the fact of her thoughts earlier on his love for his sacred golf game.

"You know what? I have to say…I am rea-ly im-pressed." She laughingly added. "I really am. Who knew?"

With the singing escapade over Etta Mae began recounting the saga of her dream.

"Now, let me finish telling my vision, or my dream. This will really get your attention,"

"You sure about that?" Donnie interjected, looking past his wife at a possible hiding place for the desired object.

"Oh, it will! Trust me." Etta Mae said also turning her attention to the source of distraction.

"Oh, believe me! Your shirt is not there." Breaking Donnie's hope. So… I was saying, I looked up, and the sky was full of clouds. But get this; the clouds were in the form of angels!"

"Angels!" Donnie shouted.

"Angels!" She repeated. "And they were not just any clouds, but they were altocumulus clouds!"

"How'd we get from dirt to angels?" Donnie asked in amusement. "And now look at 'ya… "They were alto-cu-mu-lus clouds." He said seemingly unconvinced. "Go on baby!"

"What! You still don't believe me? She asked after hearing the skepticism in his voice. "It was a dream! Ya' big dummy!

"Alright now, it does not call for all that." The beleaguered man slumped onto a nearby chair.

"Sorry, baby… but you just keep… Anyways." Etta continued. "The angels were the kind you see on Valentine cards. You know the little cherub looking ones.

And the sky was full of them! And when I looked over to my right, there was a cloud like figure sitting on a throne!"

"What-chu-say!" Now this really got the skeptic's attention. "Go ahead girl!" Donnie excitedly urged his wife. "A cloudy figure was sitting on a cloudy throne!"

"No-oo! Not like that! She said trying to clarify her meaning. "I just meant it was all composed of clouds."

His enlivened interest in the matter pleased her.

"Now mind you, I didn't get a good look at the figure, because that's when I woke up. Darn it!"

Donnie reached over to feel his wife's forehead. Her dream must've been something out of this world for her to be this worked up.

Undoubtedly, it's really taken a toll on her emotions. He reasoned. He'd never known Etta Mae to carry on in such a way. But all in all, he believed what she'd said.

Donnie knew his wife spent a lot of time reading the Bible. So why wouldn't God appear to her in a dream? After all, he'd only ribbed his 'wittle munchkin' for a little lighted humor.

He'd watched her pour over the Scriptures nearly every night of their married life. So much so, dinner would sometimes be a quick microwavable entree.

But who was complaining? Not him. After all she did put up with his golf fanaticism.

And so … He thought to himself….as the world turns. To each his own.

With this thought in mind, Donnie resigned to return to the task at hand. But the eager storyteller wasn't done.

"Don… honey, I believe I saw 'El Shaddai' sitting on His throne."

"Wow!" Was all the perplexed man could muster.

"As a cloud, now, imagine that!" It was still too much for even her to fathom. Now exhausted from it all Etta fell back on the bed curling into a fetal position.

"Like Isaiah 6 says; "I saw the Lord high and lifted up. Wow!"

Rolling onto her back, Etta Mae staring at the ceiling, began mentally replaying the sacred image in her mind once again.

I swear, the more I live with this woman the more she never ceases to amaze me. Donnie thought shaking his head in bewilderment.

I can deal with her associating everything under the sun to 'divine providence,' but I don't think I was ready for this.

"Too much, too much." He muttered bending once again sorting through the scattered clothing once again.

"What" Etta groggily inquired.

Oh…nothing." Donnie answered with his wife's mental wellbeing running through his mind. "Nothing at all. Just what was it all about? The thought of a person inviting Christ into their life but can then be distracted, allowing themselves to be turned aside thereby becoming unfit for God's Kingdom, Donnie concluded must be what Luke 9:62 is all about.

But! Donnie quickly reasoned to himself. Not my Etta! No turning back. There's no turning back for my sweet girl. She's in it for the long-haul.

Now, Dee, her sister, on the other hand… Donnie's thoughts drifted to their unexpected guest resting in the adjacent room. He thought of his sister-in-law's agnostic outlook on life.

Eventually, the search for the beloved shirt led the battle-weary soul into the walk-in closet.

"Oh, this is killing me; where is my damn shirt?" He said, a little too forcefully.

The profane outburst startled his reclining wife. She rose from the bed, but resolvedly, allowed herself to fall back once again and remained quiet.

"Well, I guess I'll just have to break in another one."

An unrestrained groan could be heard coming from the bed.

The thought of having to endure yet another 'token of luck,' was a bit disheartening.

Yet, she would indulge his only obsession repeatedly if it made her man happy. Still, the urge to taunt him was too irresistible.

"No-oo! Surely you don't mean that! Not another good luck token!"

But the intended sarcasm fell on deaf ears, because the frustrated golfer didn't bother responding to the friendly slight. He abruptly left the room.

"Oh, now my feelings are hurt!" The slighted woman shouted towards the door feigning a sorrowful demeanor. "O, boo, hoo."

"Etta Mae, what are you grumbling about? It's not as if you have to wash it or anything."

Donnie yelled from the hall.

"No, I don't have to wash it! I can't get the darn thing off 'ya long enough to wash it." She shot back.

"All I know is, when I wear that shirt, my game is really on!"

He said poking his head back into the bedroom.

"But babe, you should be able to find it by the smell alone."

"Oh, aren't we the funny one." Donnie said under his breath as he journeyed down the hall.

Etta Mae had hidden the shirt in the clothes hamper. She had plucked the smelly 'lucky charm' up by the broom handle as it lay discarded on the dining room chair.

"You, my friend are stone out of your luck, because all your karma is going down the drain."

CHAPTER
Three

The morning's commotion had awakened the Smith's house guest who had flown in unexpectedly from New York the day before. Dee, as she was referred to by her siblings, is somewhat of an agnostic.

Her religious views totally rivaled that of her siblings, Etta Mae and Cynthia, their youngest sister.

You couldn't exactly call her an atheist, because she had believed once.

Delilah Whitman sauntered into her sister's bedroom with her pink silk robe securely tied.

"Hey, Sis, I have to tell you, I'm not used to getting up this early!"

"Oh, you don't say."

"What was all the commotion about anyway?"

"Umph, apparently along with everything else, my little sister must also be a light sleeper."

Etta Mae patted the space beside her on the bed.

"Who knew you two 'early birds' got up with the chickens?"

Dee yarned, then stretched, and continued to display her irritation.

"Slamming doors, banging drawers… and what's with this darn shirt?"

"Well, excuse us for living in our home." Etta Mae exclaimed, now a tad irritated. "We didn't mean to disturb your beauty sleep."

Besides, Dee still hadn't explained to her satisfaction, the reason why she'd arrived so unexpectedly. Etta Mae got up from the bed.

"Well don't you go getting all snippy with me Miss Etta!"

Dee countered. "I'm just trying to figure out what all the noise was about."

"Sorry, Sister."

Etta Mae felt a tad regretful and only offered an apology to stave off the inevitable argument.

"I'm not usually up this early myself on a Saturday morning."

"So, why are you up?"

"I'm on call nearly every day of the week, so everyone knows it's my only day to sleep in. And you know what my Sundays bring."

"Let me guess; church."

Delilah's gaze followed her sister's retreat. Etta Mae pulled at the edge of the window shades and peered out into the morning. Her mind had once again returned to her vision.

"Earth to Etta, hel-lo." Delilah frantically snapped her fingers. "Hel-lo, I was talking to you."

"Huh… Oh, I'm sorry; you asked why I was up."

"Yep, that's what I asked."

"Mmm, well from what I can gather, I disturbed Donnie too much in bed last night… apparently."

Genuinely concerned, Dee got up, walked over and turned her sister to face her.

"Are you alright? You look a little pale. That is if a black woman can look pale!"

"What were you two doing last night anyways, knocking boots? If that's the case, I didn't hear any screaming."

She gave her sister a playful nudge. The concerned sibling was hoping to bring a little humor into the suddenly chilled room, but her humorous efforts only received a blank stare.

Etta Mae desperately wanted to oblige her sister's efforts of keeping the conversation light, but she simply was not feeling it.

"Oh, little sister you wouldn't understand."

"No? Try me; whatever it is, it appears to have you floored. You're not your old self."

"What is my old self? You haven't been around me for quite some time."

"I know, and I know I should do better."

"Yes, you should."

"I heard you tell Donnie that you had a dream, or was it more like a nightmare?"

Her sister's troubling behavior was so unlike the 'Rock of Gibraltar' Dee knew her to be. Nothing could chisel away her sister's 'porcelain veneer' coated emotions.

Delilah hadn't seen her eldest sister in such a state of wonderment since she'd learned of Grams pending home going.

She retreated back to the bed, leaving Etta Mae to stare out the window. The memory of their beloved grandmother's departure came to the forefront of her mind.

It had been a cold, rainy day in December 1985. She and her siblings had all gathered around their grandmother's hospital bed with each of their minds absorbed in loving memories.

"Goodbye, Grams, I love you." Delilah had whispered.

"Tell Mom and Pop hello for us." Cynthia had said pass the knot in her throat.

Grams had smiled and had sought Etta Mae's face out of the three girls. The dying matriarch had called her name with a barely audible voice.

"Et-Etta Mae?"

'Yes, Grams? I'm-we're here, we're all here." Etta Mae had said, with choking tears. The three sisters had taken hold of the feeble hands.

"It's up to you now… Etta Ma-Mae." The dying woman had stammered. "I tried to do my best by each of you." (Cough) "It's up to you now… take care of your sisters. (Cough, cough) It's time for me to go. I-I am rea-dy."

Afterwards, Grams had focused her eyes on the ceiling. She had smiled, and with one last breath had closed her eyes.

Torrential flood gates had opened, as personal dams burst forth. The hospital room had been filled with sobs. They held and comforted each other for a long time.

The unusually harsh North Carolina winter had been hazardous to their grandmother's fragile health. Her health had been spiraling downhill for quite some time.

She had attended a close friend's funeral in a cold rain and had ended up with bronchial pneumonia.

The pneumonia had taken a toll on her weak lungs and she hadn't possessed the stamina to pull through.

Dee thought back on the tales her grandmother would tell them of her life.

Beulah Eileen Collins was their paternal grandmother's name. She had been born in Cartersville, a small town in North Carolina that boasted of being a small college town.

One day her husband, Thaddeus, had assumed he was only suffering with a bad case of indigestion, and had died on his railroad job while inspecting tracks.

However, the cause of death was later diagnosed as complications of an enlarged heart.

Beulah had reared her only son, James Anthony Collins alone, while earning a living as a second-grade teacher.

Greenbrier Elementary School sat at the far end of a one-way street, surrounded by homes that once sported green lawns and picket fences.

The small town of 30,000 was located near the white sands of the Neuse River, named after the Neusioks, an American Indian tribe.

Their grandmother had told the girls tales of how the river was prone to extremes in its flow carriage, and often escaped its banks during wet periods.

When it was reduced to a trickle in the dry season, the river could be forded on foot.

Their grandfather, she had said would often go fishing when the water was at its normal level.

Unemployment had run high. The upkeep of the homes in the town reflected the state of the economy at the time.

Many of the prominent blacks had left town to venture north to cities such as D.C., or Baltimore.

The less educated factory workers were left to supply the makeup of the neighborhood.

'James, their father, affectionately known as 'Jimmie,' was a fragile child. He had been prone to wheezing and catching colds at the drop of a hat.

So, Beulah, ever the doting mother, would dress her delicate son in double layers in the winter.

A knitted white cap, mittens, galoshes and a little blue snow suit served as his protected armor. A blue and white scarf wrapped up to his nose completed the ensemble.

On wintry days little Jimmie would often resemble a well-dressed snow man. The attire was so cumbersome their father would barely be able to lower his arms.

As a result, Jimmie learned to answer to the name of 'Michelin Boy.'

He spent many days watching from the sideline, longing to join in the fun with the neighborhood boys.

After graduating from Dunn High School, James had gone on to attend the College of Cartersville.

Any thought of going away to school was clearly out of the question. Beulah wasn't about to allow her darling, only child to get away from her unfaltering scrutiny.

Donna Elaine Garrett had come into the life of James Collins one rainy day while the two dodged a sudden downpour.

The Devereaux Carter Library was an ideal place to study as it remained opened at least twelve hours daily. Many a late night study sessions had taken place during semester finals.

Donna's favorite secluded table had been in the non-fiction section of the library. The library had served as a refuge.

Gretchen, her roommate's active social life, often left Donna no recourse, but to hang out at the only spot that afforded her the peace and quiet to read.

She would lovingly run her fingers along the many books, and then settle on a title that caught her interest. The romantic escapades of Gretchen had resulted in Donna being well read.

Jimmie had sat at the table in the corner and had sneezed into his sleeve.

"Bless you." A familiar female voice had said from between the row of books.

He'd heard that voice before in his 2:00 English Comp class. It belonged to a beautiful olive-skinned young woman who sat about three rows behind him.

He could listen to it all day; her voice had a way of sending chills down his spine.

As fate would have it, that chance meeting on a rainy autumn afternoon, had been the beginning of a whirlwind romance that eventually led to their marriage.

Subsequently, three darling daughters had made their union complete.

Unfortunately, their parents had died tragically in a plane crash. It had been a devastating loss for them all. The widow had taken the three sisters in to her home.

James and Donna Collins had been fun, and loving parents, who always spent quality time with their daughters.

James, at first, had wished for a son, but after having his first daughter, he couldn't have loved the four ladies in his life more.

Etta Mae, being the oldest of the three sisters had taken to mothering her two younger sisters with zeal, after the loss of their loving parents.

Dee, the middle child, had resorted to finding outlets to cope with her grief.

She had tried finding solace in the homes of girlfriends by imagining she was part of a real family.

The youngest of the three girls was Cynthia, a silent shadow of a daughter, with a quiet demeanor.

Of the three sisters, Cynthia looked most like their mother; olive skin with a narrow nose set on a chiseled face with prominent cheek bones and hooded eyelids. Her shoulder length hair was often worn flipped at the ends.

Growing up, Cynthia had focused her full attention on finding the answer to the age-old question.

"Why would a God who was all loving allow such a bad thing to happen to such 'good people' as her Mom and Dad?"

She would ask her grandmother and anyone else she thought would know the answer.

Etta Mae used to say she could only hope Cynthia's answer would be found in her Doctor of Theological Studies.

The recapture of Dee's cherished childhood memories are abruptly halted as Etta Mae turned from the window.

On second thought, she had decided to share the morning's escapade with her sibling.

"Sister, you're not going to believe this, but I had the most amazing vision this morning."

"You did?"

"You do know God is not limited to how He speaks, don't you?"

The look of skepticism on her sister's face did little to dispel her enthusiasm.

"I believe it was a vision, or maybe I was just dreaming, who can say. I may have been awake during it all. You never know."

"No, I wouldn't know." Dee sarcastically stated. "I haven't spoken to Him, and He certainly hasn't said a thing to me!"

She was overcome with frustration. The air of lightheartedness was dampened by the discussion of religion.

Etta Mae felt hurt and looked at her sister with disbelief. The passing of time it seemed hadn't erased the gravity of her wayward sister's denial of the 'Creator.'

"Well, I'm just glad He speaks to me. I don't know how you can live without Him."

She asked her sister an emotionally charged question.

"Exactly, how do you cope?"

"Oh, I manage just nicely thank you."

Now that the torrent of emotion had been released, there was no holding back.

"I believe you and Cynthia have enough religion, 'quote-unquote,' for the three of us. You two live eat and breathe God.

Hallelujah this and *hallelujah* that. You can't even carry on a decent conversation without hearing God said, or God revealed."

Etta Mae knew it would be fruitless to interject with her sister in this frame of mind, so she only listened.

"What had happened to the sweet little girl who used to hold Grams hand so tightly in church? Their grandmother would have to pry the fingers loose in order to clap."

"She had believed once, so she's bound to believe again." Etta Mae resolved herself into thinking. She returned to the topic of her dream.

"I wonder what He was saying, though. Cynthia should be able to tell me. I'm going to call her today."

Dee decided to take advantage of her brother-in-law's entrance.

"Brother-n-law, is your wife always like this in the morning? Then if that's the case, I surely feel sorry for you."

Donnie looked at the sisters with amusement; he smiled and patted his wife's head.

"Have you heard about her angels?"

"My baby got the 'hook up' to heaven!" Donnie jovially shouted.

"Dee… I wish you could've heard her last night. I know she was asleep, but it was as if she was out of this world!"

"Say what? "The 'devil's advocate' inquired in anticipation.

"What was she saying, or how was she acting?"

"Yes, Lord, praise God!" And get this."

Donnie responded with acute animation after realizing he had everyone's full attention.

"And then she started speaking some gibberish." He wiped the sweat from his forehead.

"It scared the heck out of me."

Etta Mae looked on as the two are caught up in their comedic banter at her expense.

"Oooh! I bet you were about to crap your pants!"

"Heck, ye-ah! I jumped up so fast and looked at her."

He continued his charade while his sister-in-law was overcome with laughter.

"And then she started waving her hands and singing."

He went even further to add how he thought his love may have become possessed.

"I'm just glad I made it out alive, heck, I thought her head was fixing to spin around and spit out green slime!"

"You're crazy, and you say she was singing?"

Dee was overcome with uncontrollable laughter as she hung on to the stand-up comic's every word.

"So you got yourself a midnight serenade, I bet that freaked you out."

"Yep, you heard me, she was singing, so I said…What 'da hell?"

The two slapped each other a high five, but, the caring husband was truly concerned. He had found the night's happenings a bit unnerving.

"And check this out; this morning she believes she saw *God Almighty.*"

"Now that's deep." Dee used the back of her hand to wipe away tears of laughter.

Donnie was only being amusing for her sake. He had often witnessed his wife being caught up 'in the spirit.'

God is so real to him also. He studied the 'Word' in his own way and his own time.

Etta Mae doesn't know the extent of his knowledge. His 'better half' naturally assumed the game of golf was more important to him than his faith.

"Hey, Bro-law, maybe if you had stayed in bed long enough, some of that holiness would've rubbed off on you."

Donnie stole a quick glance at his silent wife in time to see a hurtful look come over her face. Finally, he contended, enough was enough, so he decided to drop the subject.

He gave his wife a quick hug of reassurance, but Dee kept the jovial banter going.

"So that's why you decided to go golfing, aye?"

She gave him a slight punch on the shoulder with her fist.

"And what's up with this shirt you've been looking high and low for?"

The mention of the sacred icon is disquieting to Etta Mae, and a feeling of foreboding showed on her face.

The instigating sibling saw it as an opportunity to get a rise from her sister. She looked pointedly at Etta Mae and went on to ask Donnie.

"Do you really believe it's a 'good luck' charm, or did you just have 'wifey' here lay anointed hands on it?"

"I have to tell you; I'm finding you two to be some real characters."

"We're characters?"

Etta Mae was miffed and hurt by the dialogue and decided to put a stop to it.

"So, if you two are finished! She said a little too sarcastically. "I would like to say, I know I'm not crazy so you two can laugh all you want, but my '*Daddy*' doesn't show Himself to just any and everybody!"

"Ah… babe, no one is thinking you're losing it; huh Dee?"

Donnie gave his partner-in-crime a sly wink, but she simply smirked and looked down at the floor.

"Honey, Dee didn't mean what she said, or the way she said it for that matter."

He glanced at the suddenly quiet culprit for confirmation.

"At least I hope she didn't."

His sister-in-law did little to reassure him, so he added yet another explanation.

"We just thought it all to be a little strange, that's all."

"Donnie LeRoy! I can't believe you! You of all people should know me by now. You know when it comes to the Gospel, I don't play!"

Donnie sensed the seriousness in his wife's voice and tried his hand at apologizing. He grabbed his love around her waist and pulled her close. He kissed her on the forehead and pressed her face into his chest.

"Oh, I'm sorry you felt I wasn't taking you serious, honey."

The repenting husband pressed his lips to his wife's head and warmly muttered.

"Forgive me for acting a fool. And yes, I can see this means a lot to you."

Dee watched the two with indifference but did not bother offering any show of compassion.

"If you two could just have a Jesus encounter … just once!"

Etta Mae shouted as she tearfully pulled away from her repenting spouse. Donnie's arms dropped to his side in defeat. Shrugging his shoulders in bewilderment.

"Well, I don't know about y'all, but I think I hear a 9-iron calling my name. So, I'm going to take my leave… ladies."

He leaned over to kiss his wife once again before leaving the room.

"You two ladies have a nice day."

Etta Mae watched him leave, blatantly wishing he would become more adamant in his faith walk.

He occasionally attended Wednesday night Bible study at Shiloh Baptist Church, often sitting quietly, hopefully, she thought absorbing the lesson.

She had no doubt that her husband was a true believer, much unlike her sister, of whom she hadn't fully given up hope.

"Do you know what Dee?"

"Don't say it, because you know I don't want to hear it."

Highly annoyed, the agitated lass got up from the bed and left the room in a huff.

"Oh well, not to worry, today is a new day. "This is the day that the Lord has made, and I *will* rejoice, and I *will* be glad in it!" Etta Mae clarified it by shouting it out loud.

With this self-declaration, she climbed back into her California King bed, snuggled under the covers, and fell fast asleep; blessedly assured in her soul salvation.

The repenting spouse highly anticipated the start of his golf game. The old adrenalin rush began as soon as he gently placed his new stand-alone golf bag in the trunk of his car.

The new bag was the top of the line and was most ideal for the golfer who wanted a stylish look.

The bag's feature of a 6-Way top was the deciding factor. It boasted of having five-pockets with a water bottle sleeve, and the Pivot dual shoulder strap, which made it more comfortable to carry.

He hadn't wanted to replace his favorite driving iron, or the well-worn clubs. Their familiarity was too much to his liking.

Donnie's day was set, he felt equipped to do a little damage other than the fact of missing his 'lucky icon.'

He made his way around the new Audi Sedan he'd purchased two months earlier for his wife. The pewter gray four door sedan remained stationary for the most part, unless she was going to church, or shopping.

It wasn't that his wife hadn't appreciated the generous gift, but for everyday use, she'd preferred driving the old, dark green Toyota Camry.

Donnie chalked it up to her simply having an 'only use the best china for festive occasions' syndrome.

Saturdays were reserved for house cleaning. It was also the best day to chat with her 'bestie' and next door neighbor, Tonika Gibbons.

He had to chuckle when he had once overheard them discussing the price of gas.

"Gir-rl did you see the price of gas has gone to $4.95 a gallon?" Etta Mae had asked. "It just doesn't make any sense."

However, Tonika's mind had been far from the price of gas. She had already supposed early on, the crucial oil spill had driven the price of gas sky high. So to her it wasn't too surprising.

"Good, then maybe my significant other's pockets are lighter, after filling up that 'pimped out' ride of his."

She'd recalled how Josh had filled his 'gas guzzler' on Wednesday, but hadn't complained one bit about the astronomical price of the 'gold liquid.'

"Oh, well." Etta Mae had simply said.

Donnie had noticed his neighbor hadn't said "my better half, nor had she referred to 'my husband' in the conversation."

Although, she wasn't ready to discuss her problems at home, Tonika knew she'd better add clarity to her recent comment.

"He just loves that ride of his… sometimes, I think more than me. Anyhow, I'm thinking about parking my ride, and footing it to where I need to go."

"Now, that's a joke." Donnie had thought to himself. "Not as long as my wife is around, she won't have to foot it."

He dearly enjoyed ribbing his neighbor as she had a keen sense of humor.

The one thing that could undoubtedly antagonize his friend to no end was to screw up her name.

"Sharmika, Chiquita, and especially, Tomika, were just a few of the mispronunciation he'd jokingly use.

Needless to say, her temper would spike to the utmost, amusing him to no end.

Life hadn't been too kind to her when he and his wife had first encountered her. Her first husband Jamal, a tall, robust, athletic, figure of a man had left her and an infant son high and dry.

Donnie was pleased his wife spent time with Tonika. As a matter of fact, an imminent conversion any day wouldn't surprise him in the least.

Backing his black Buick Regal out of the driveway, the man's mind was filled with many thoughts.

Shucks, as far as that goes, even if my saucy sister-in-law would stick around long enough, I'm almost certain her faithless stance on religion would follow suit.

He casually glanced over his shoulder in time to see Josh, his neighbor putting a suitcase in the trunk of his car. His wife could be seen through the front window wiping tears away.

"Don't tell me this one is on the run too. What's with that woman that she can't keep her man?"

Donnie honked his horn, and waved to Josh. However, the friendly gesture was not returned. He drove off puzzled by it all.

"Looks like my wife's shoulder will be soaked today with her friend's salty tears." He thought.

As he drove along, Donnie wondered how things would go with his sister-in-law being in the house.

"No doubt my kindhearted, 'love of my life' is sure to have her hands full."

But he also knew his wife to be a mighty fortress. All advice she would give either of them would be 'divine wisdom', no question about it.

Somehow just basking in the marvelous job she'd done rearing their only daughter, Dr. Janet Beulah Singleton, a clinical psychologist was enough to keep her in a everlasting glow non-stop.

Janet lived in Hawaii with her husband of seven years, Geoffrey, a general practitioner. It looked as though no grandkids were on the horizon given the pursuit of achieving lucrative careers. But! One can hope can't he.? n. The grandfather want-a-be thought to himself.

His wife, on the other hand, had simply resolved never to pressure the young couple in their decision making in that department.

"It's their decision alone to make." She would duly note.

Yep! That wife of mine it seems is capable of handling life's little obstacles it all with insurmountable patience but as for me, the golf range awaits.

"If I hit it right, it's a slice, if I hit left, it's a hook. If I hit it straight... then it's a miracle!"

"Mr. Woods eat your heart out!" He yelled into the air.

The hard-core golfer pressed his right foot a little harder on the gas pedal, sending the smooth ride slicing through the morning air.

CHAPTER
Four

....

The beige suede couch still held Josh's imprint where he had slept the night before. He had later returned after an abrupt departure. Neither he nor his broken-hearted spouse had sought the other out.

Tonika had heard him rise very early. He had retrieved the clothes from the floor where she had angrily thrown them after emptying drawers, and yanking clothes off their hangers.

"Get out you bastard!" she had screamed. "I don't ever want to see your cheating face around here ever again!"

Closet doors slammed shut, drawers opened and closed as Josh had gone about collecting his belongings.

He had reluctantly entered the bedroom to retrieve other personal items. She had sat on their bed and silently watched.

"I'll come back for the rest of my stuff when I find a place."

Tonika had followed him into the living room without saying a word.

She had stood at the window with tears streaming down her face, and watched as the candy-apple red, standard 10th Anniversary Trans Am sped away with tires squealing.

She had also watched as her neighbor backed his all too familiar black sedan out onto the street.

The puzzled look on his face hadn't gone unnoticed after having been slighted by Josh. There had definitely been a look of concern on his usually jovial face.

All in all, Tonika loved being married. She loved the thought of coming home to a traditional family; a home with a husband and that all too important 1.1child the way God designed a family to be.

"What was that scripture again?" She pondered. "Oh I know. "When a man findeth a wife, he findeth a good thing."

"Josh had certainly found himself a good 'thang' when he'd found her, because a good 'thang' she was."

She chuckled at her Ebonic slang, as she made her way into the kitchen.

"What life factors had driven the men in her life away?"

A state of depression had over shadowed Jamal after their loss. She reasoned, but with Josh...there was no excuse. Tears flowed once again.

"Mom, can I... may I have a bowl of frosted cereal?"

Ten-year old Ashad rubbed his growling belly as he ventured into the kitchen.

"Mom! Are you okay?"

The young boy rushed over to his mother and grasped her arm to turn her towards him. Before she turned around Tonika managed to put on her best happy face.

When she faced her gangly, curly haired son, the mindful mother couldn't help but notice how much shorter her son's blue flannel 'pj's she'd recently purchased, now rose above his slender ankles.

"Oh, hey baby, surely, you can have as much cereal as you like. Here, let me get it down for you."

She retrieved the cereal from the overhead cupboard and poured her rambunctious son a hefty bowl of his favorite breakfast. She sat the box down in front of him, clearly knowing that one bowl would never be enough.

A warm motherly glow descended from the top of her head down to the tips of her toes.

The doting mother's chest swelled with pride at the thought of having reared such a handsome, well-mannered child.

Ashad was the spitting image of his Samoan father. She watched each day as little traits of Jamal emerged in her son. The way his ears moved when a broad smile swept across his face.

Tonika would lovingly pull at the dancing ears, which often resulted in much mother–son bonding. She turned to cradle his infantile face in both hands, hoping to plant a quick peck onto his cheek.

"Mein liebschen! Ich liebe dich!"

She uttered in her German mother's native tongue. Ashad squirmed and ducked his head to avoid the motherly smothering.

"Love you too, Mommy." He said, after he finally allowed her kisses to land.

She headed into the living room, afterwards. Yesterday's mail lay on the coffee table where she'd plopped it down.

As she sorted through the junk mail and the never ending bills, Tonika's heart pumped wildly as she held an envelope from her doctor.

She'd gone for her annual check-up and mammogram last week. Diabetes tended to run in her immediate family, so he'd extracted blood samples.

"Oh, this must be the results of my blood test. I sure pray I don't have diabetes."

Tonika slid her index finger under the envelope's flap. Her eyes widened as she read the words on the page.

Your 'T' cell count…. Tonika fainted.

CHAPTER
Five

....

Etta Mae had slept for more than three hours. Finally, she awakened. Stretching in bed, she rose slowly and tied her favorite blue chenille robe loosely around her waist.

Making her way down the hall to the kitchen, the backless navy velour house shoes' making a slap, slap, slap sound on the wooden floor cutting into the home's now silent atmosphere.

"Blessed assurance, Jesus is mine, oh what a foretaste of glory divine... Wow!" She said aloud. "Now that song is stuck in my head. Sister Brown must surely be wearing off on me."

"But, *praise the Lord anyhow!* It's a darn good feeling to know that He's *mine,* and I'm truly *His.* Amen!"

Her steps quickened as her nose followed the aroma of the freshly brewed coffee, thanks to her thoughtful husband.

She poured a cup of the aromatic brew and settled down at the granite kitchen counter.

The hot liquid was all she could handle substance-wise; thanks to a nervous stomach. She looked around the well-kept home, pleased with her handiwork.

The coordinating shades of ivory and mocha color scheme enhanced the décor of the adjoining rooms. Etta Mae loved her life and her home.

The Smiths called Chauncey, New Jersey, home. The neighborhood was a makeup of tri-level and ranch style homes lined on forested streets.

Staunch oak and sycamore trees dating back to the Pre-Civil War era, stood as if watchful guardians over each dwelling.

The houses varied in strict color patterns of taupe, kelly-green, brown, or muted gold set by the neighborhood association.

Jeremiah Joyner was the only resident who'd dared to challenge the rule, by painting his brown tri-level a bright lemon yellow. Needless to say, the hideous color was a major eye sore.

However, the defiant home owner soon came in line after the stiff penaltyhe'dincurred.

The Smiths lived in a 1,900 square foot, taupe three-bedroom ranch-home. Dresden blue shutters framed the casement windows. French doors led out to a two tiered deck.

She casually scanned the 'L' shaped living/dining rooms from where she sat. The contented homemaker made a mental note to put her dust buster and vacuum cleaner to good use sometime soon.

Drying dishes left in a rack was the domestic vigilante's number one pet peeve, thankfully, none could be seen.

The front and back yards were the 'preist' of the household's pride and joy. The back yard's well-manicured sloped lawn was enclosed by a shellacked four foot high wooden fence.

A myriad of small, colorful fish swam nonchalantly in a bubbling man-made pond that was surrounded by an array of colorful blosoms. He would lovingly tend to his horticultural masterpiece on Saturdays after a morning spent at the range.

Etta Mae moved to the solid mahogany dining table after retrieving her Bible from the credenza. She'd wanted to complete the final chapters of the Gospel of John for some time now.

Jesus' many spoken words and presence throughout the entire book was extremely inspiring, to say the least.

But, for some reason or other she just couldn't concentrate. For one thing her sister's troubling attitude continued to plague her thoughts.

Etta Mae inadvertently turned to a book other than John's. Her eyes fell on Hebrews, Chapter 12.

"Hum mm, now would you look at that? It says here;*"Therefore, we are surrounded by such a great cloud of witnesses…"*

"Now, how co-incidental is that? First, I dream of clouds as to what I thought to be angels, and here I turn to this scripture. Hum mm, cloud of witnesses… hum mm."

"I just wonder if some of those witnesses weren't Peter, or Paul, *or Paul, or Mary. Ha, ha, ha!*

Etta Mae laughed at her own pun.

"Peter, Paul and Mary! *Ha, ha, ha!*"

Then another thought registered.

"Say…what if Mommy, Daddy and my dear, dear grandmother were among those clouds?"

The once joyous demeanor was soon overshadowed with solemn memories.

"Thanks for watching out guys. And Grams, I'm trying to keep all my promises I made to you…I'm trying with all my heart."

A lone tear trickled down her saddened face. The forlorn daughter sat deep in thought. Due to the high level of stress she had been experiencing lately, Etta Mae had inadvertently chewed the top of her pen to a pulp. She grabbed a tissue to wipe the ink smudge from her lip.

Her well-rested sister entered the kitchen about that time, wearing a bright floral, silk lounge ensemble. Etta Mae knew the ensemble could cost as much as her monthly car notes.

The sound of her black high heeled mules, topped with a puff of black fur was muffed on the crème Berber carpet. The elite socialite was always meticulous in her attire.

The shoulder length mane was swept up into a stylish French roll. Full lips as moist as a rose touched with a hint of morning dew sparkled from the red lip gloss she'd painstakingly applied.

Wondering if Etta Mae was feeling any better, Dee cast a quick glance her sister's direction before picking up a glossy magazine from the coffee table, than she had earlier. She wanted to ease the tension that was so evident. She decided to draw her sister into a conversation.

"Hey, Sissy… what are you reading?"

Etta Mae held up her Bible without bothering to look up, or to speak.

"Oh, I should've known it was the 'Good Book.' I don't know why I even asked?"

"Well, why did you? I wouldn't want to surprise you or anything. You know what I mean?"

Yes, Dee knew what she meant. She'd seen and heard it all before.

"You remind me so much of Grams." Dee said."Out of us three girls, she definitely rubbed off on you."

"Yep, you got that right. I listened, where as you…."

Etta Mae does not finish the sentence; not caring to rehash the morning's discussion.

"Yeah, yeah." Dee merely waved her hand in a gesture to dismiss the remark.

"And I know what you're about to say. And I'm about to say this; "I'll give my life to your Jesus. Maybe… *like tomorrow.*"

Nonchalantly, continuing to flip through the magazine, suddenly an interesting article catches her attention.

"Look at this!" She exclaimed. "Hear ye, hear ye, straight from the headlines! Preacher has reached a settlement!"

Etta Mae focused more intently on the scriptures before her. She'd read the magazine article last week, and had thought at the time, how it made being able to witness to the lost more detrimental.

Needless to say, her sister's condescending attitude had proven that same fact to be true.

"It seems he'd been enticing young women with fancy cars and gaudy jewelry for a little tete-a-tete!"

Etta Mae willed herself to stay composed. If her condescending sibling felt her agnostic views was justified by the devious actions of a few fallen clergy, then so be it.

However, it would benefit her to know that when *all* stand before the 'King,' he or she will only give account for his or her, good or bad deeds. And no one else's.

"*Ha, ha, ha!*" Dee had let out a hefty laugh.

"Apparently, they weren't having the private conversations as that ole rat had claimed. It says here the women sued his old butt for making sexual advances toward them. *Ha, ha, ha!*"

"Now, that's just great, that's all I needed. The queen of 'I don't believe' just had to read that one darn article." Etta Mae thought to herself.

"I'm glad that article is bringing you so much joy, but I for one, fail to see the humor in it."

"That's not surprising; you wouldn't."

Etta Mae braced herself for the old "that's the reason I don't go to church," plus the old "nothing but a bunch of hypocrites," speech.

As it was, the many revelers she had approached for the purpose of witnessing would often throw the hellish declaration back at her.

Along with; "why should I come and give that old highfalutin preacher my hard earned money?"

Then they would often add; "Just so he can live like a king. Besides, you guys are doing the same thing in church as we're doing out here."

Pastor Grantham had preached about the value of self-control. One of the nine fruit of the 'Spirit' a few weeks ago.

"The flesh or the carnal mind was restless and wanted control over our lives. It is deceptive and causes the people of God to fall prey to all kinds of temptations.

Only the 'Spirit of God' can give one the power to take charge over one's flesh." Pastor had also said.

Etta Mae recalled thinking how close his sermon paralleled with what was happening to the unfortunate soul mentioned in the article.

Dee devoured the article with fervor. She wasn't done digging her claws into her devout sister's righteous stance.

This article could undoubtedly be the arsenal she needed to use in her defense.

"I know you follow all those mega guys, so I know you know the preacher they're talking about here."

"Oh no, here it comes." Etta Mae groaned within herself.

"This is the one with custom made suits, and drives around in that white Bentley down there in good ole Alabama."

"That's not saying much. That could be any of them. It would appear money has become the idol of the day. Maybe, that's the reason behind this very scandal."

"True, true, but you know what?" Dee went on, absently snapping her fingers.

"Oh, here it is! Reverend Travis Thornton. That's his name. And I know you know him. Or, at least heard of him."

"Uh huh, I know him." Etta Mae interjected in a low voice. "And that's really too bad."

She felt a tightening in her stomach. The fact that a scandal such as this even came about sickened her to the core.

"Chalk one up for the devil." Etta Mae offered no further comment, as she didn't care to give credence to the article.

"Spare me, *please...* that's a man of God all right."

Dee bellowed, still deeply engrossed in the article.

"So, as it turns out the '*man* of the cloth' is no better than the rest of the world's damn ball busters!"

Etta Mae's highlighter fell to the floor. Her tingling 'spider sense' signaled there was more to her sister's outburst than the article.

"What did you say?" She asked. "Sistah-Girl, can I tell you that this book say's; *"To be in the world, but not of the world."*

"So I just try real hard to keep my *"mind on things above, and not beneath."* Now do you feel me?"

"Yes, O' holy one, I feel you." She mockingly extended her hands and bowed. And I can see you're about to spread those glorious wings and depart this world. So, I'll just concede."

"Don't go getting cute with me, Missy. And let me tell you something!"

"Go ahead, preacher-woman, tell me!" Dee defiantly shouted.

"I'm secure in my walk with the Lord." Etta shouted back. *"But,* can you say that?"

"Oh! Enough with the sermons already! Okay?"

Etta Mae felt a little disappointed for having responded so strongly.

Somehow knowing if Dee was to ever return to her faith, it wouldn't be by her sounding 'holier than thou.' So, she backed off a bit.

"*Okay,* but I was about to let you have it with both barrels blazing."

"Well thank you for mercy." Dee humorously said. Then she changed the subject to something different all together.

"Me and this woman were talking on the plane..."

"And just what were you two talking about?"

"Oh, nothing much, we just struck up a conversation about an article she was reading. The article mentioned how laws are being passed that's changing the sanctity of marriage."

"Oh? And did you tell that woman on the plane you're on husband number... let's see..." Etta Mae said as she began finger counting. "Seven!"

"No, I didn't! Now, why would I tell a complete stranger my business? And it's not even seven, thank you very much." Dee shouted defensively. "And if it was what would be so wrong with it? At least I married them!"

"Yeah, you married, and married, and married them. Child, if it wasn't seven, I know It had to be at least six."

"Think what you like, but I do have something to show for my troubles."

Dee said. Proudly flaunting the humongous gemstone adorning her left ring finger.

"Okay, okay, nice rock if I do say so myself."

Actually the enormous gem had caught Etta Mae's eye when she met her sister at the airport. She couldn't help but be impressed with its size.

"So, I see diamonds really are a girl's best friend."

"Remember you said it and not me." Dee brazenly polished the rock on her silk top.

"Yes, and if I recall... most of your husbands were way older than you." Etta Mae continued while stifling a laugh. "And from the looks of it, you didn't walk away from those old 'coots' empty handed!"

Raising her hand high in the air, once again eyeing the bobble, the well pleased socialite said to her awe-struck sister. "Honey, you haven't even lied."

The banter between the two sisters had taken on a lighter air. Etta Mae was grateful and continued ribbing Dee.

"Yes, because you certainly couldn't have been after them for their looks!"

"Well now, I wouldn't go so far as to say that. Even if they were a tad bit my senior.

Of course, looks are not everything you know, but girl… it sure does help!"

Hysterical laughter filled the room; a welcomed relief from the early morning's tension.

"I'm surprised at you. Grams never could get you to eat prunes." Etta Mae said after composing herself.

"You use to say with your face all wrinkled up, and waving them away; "No, I don't like them 'cause they're all wrinkly!'"

Rowdy laughter exploded once again, followed by a long silence. Finally, Dee broke into Etta Mae's thoughts.

"Speaking of Grams, have you heard from our little sister? I figure she's like you; out saving the world."

"Oh, sure, Cyndi called me last week. She said she'd tried calling you, but hadn't been able to reach you."

"Dang it, I hate I missed her call."

"I guess she was calling to tell you, she was going out to visit Janet and Geoffrey for a week. Of course, she should be back home by now."

"That's wonderful, the poor thing probably needed to get away from the 'rat race' for a while."

"I'm sure she enjoyed herself. And you can well bet Janet would've made sure of that.

"Well, if that's the case, then I have to get out to Hawaii myself one of these days. Maybe that's where I should've gone before coming here."

Oh, who was she kidding? Dee thought to herself, fully knowing there was no better place to be at this stage in her life than with her alternate mother. Her 'Big Sis, Etta Mae.

Though, for reasons unknown, she had been shunning their sisterly embrace.

"Perhaps, if I don't think about 'the problem,' then I don't have to deal with 'the problem,' until I'm ready to share it." She thought.

"I'm sure glad my baby girl found her a good one." Etta Mae said. "Those two are sure to grow old together."

"And just how's my sweet 'niecy' doing?"

"They're doing just peachie, and thank you for asking."

Dee caught the hidden insinuation in her sister's voice. She knew she should do better with keeping contact with her relatives, but her hectic New York life wouldn't permit it. She made a mental note to remedy that in the near future.

"I'm telling you girl, older gentleman can be all that and then some. And you're talking to someone who knows. Besides, Viagra is always on the bedside table."

"Viagra! Etta Mae asked in astonishment. "Girl, do you mean all your husbands needed that stuff?"

"No...I wouldn't say all."

Dee's declaration presented another opportunity to speak on the Bible. And Etta Mae, not to disappoint, taking full advantage of it said.

"You know... in biblical times, when God gave men the '*hook up*, so to speak, I'm here to tell you, they were *hooked up*! Just ask Moses and Abraham!"

"Sister! You never cease to amaze me. I swear!"

Dee merely shook her head.

"God restored their virility so they kept right on fathering children even after their bodies became prunes."

"Yes, I'm sure they did, but those women probably didn't have to look at their old puny butts either."

Dee said this to take the seriousness out of Etta Mae's comment.

The irony of her elder sibling constantly sneaking Bible lessons into their conversations annoyed her to the 'umph' degree.

"It's not like they romanced the women, or anything." Dee offered."They, the women I mean, probably figured it was just their wifely duties. You see what I'm saying?"

For an instant, Etta Mae was speechless. She'd never thought of it in that context. A shudder ran through her body, just picturing the sexual exploits her sister's astute observation had conjured up.

"It's just like I said, you got to be pleasing to the ole' eyes to touch this!" Dee said, pointing to her womanly treasure.

"Oh! I'm sorry Dee, what were you saying?"

"Where's your mind now? Weren't you listening? I was saying a man has to be pleasing to these eyes before he can. Oh, never mind!"

"Girlfriend, that stuff's old school, because nowadays a woman takes her man at face value."

"And again, I say, it does help. Girl, you have to wake up to that image. And luckily none of mine wore dentures."

"So all seven of them had their own teeth, huh?"

"All *thirty-two* of those muggs, and I made darn sure of that."

Dee mockingly pulled at her front teeth.

"And there you go with that darn seven again. Now I told you, it wasn't seven! It was six. And the last one, Damien, is much younger than any of them."

The two sisters are enjoying their easy chatter. Etta Mae recalled how short her sister's attention span was on settling down to one man, but like she said, at least she married them.

"So, what happened, the Viagra stopped working? Come on talk to me, Sistah-Girl."

"Etta Mae, stop it! You are so bad."

"I bet you thought you were safe with an old man, 'cause with the young handsome dudes, more often than not the more he's in love with Emma, with Sue, or Mary Jane.

Oh, and don't forget nowadays, with Tom, Dick and just maybe Harry."

While striving to keep a straight face Dee flinch at the accuracy of her sister's words hitting her in the pit of her stomach.

"Alright now …I don't know about you but an ugly man can't do a thing for me!"

"Well, after seven husbands…."

"Etta Mae! You're pissing me off now. Stop it with the seven husband bull!"

"Awww…I'm just messing with you girl. Good grief! You talk about someone being touchy. Are you PMSing or something?"

"Yes I am, if that's what you want to call it. I appreciate your concern, but enough is enough! My Goodness!"

Etta Mae now sat in silence.

After much soul searching, Dee felt ready to open up. At least that would release all the built up pressure.

After all, growing up, her big sister had been the rock she and Cynthia had leaned on throughout their childhood, and even into adulthood.

Just that thought alone had helped to bring about her decision. As painful as it was going to be, she felt she had to go through with the divorce.

"Shucks, it's because of a good looking man that I'm in this mess now. Biggest mistake I ever made in all my marriages."

"What was that baby?"

Etta Mae asked, elated, the lid was finally off the box. Speedily closing the space between them she lovingly wrapped her hurting sister in a motherly embrace.

"Come here, baby… talk to me. How can Big Sis help?"

To her surprise, the once distraught woman pulled away.

Delilah had already concluded that divorce was her only option.

"I'm sure enough going to dance a jig when this one is over."

"So you are going through with another divorce?" Etta Mae inquired. "I just thought you were being your melodramatic self, as usual."

"Yes, I am, and I'm dead serious."

"Sister, are you sure about this?"

When her sister first stepped off the plane she could tell there was a major crisis brewing.

"Honey, I'm just as sure as I am of being black. And as you can surely see, I am black!"

"Well you're sure then, because you sure are.

"Oh, just stop it! I didn't know you were so bad." Dee said finding another laugh within her.

"Well you went there."

"Oh, by the way, thanks for putting up with me for a few days, until I get my bearings."

Dee, pulling out a bejeweled compact from her pocket checked her flawless makeup.

Satisfied everything was in order she settled down to finish reading the magazine.

"You know you're welcome here anytime, honey. "Mi casa; su casa!"

Etta Mae said reassuringly reaching over to pat her sister's hand.

Since Dee had opened the way for discussion, the opportunist decided she would dig a little deeper into the matter.

"Oh yeah, you never did say what the cause of all this was about. What did Damien do? Or, maybe I should be asking; what did you do? You cast off men quicker than—"

"*Quicker than what Etta?* You know you just keep on pushing it!"

"I-I'm just concerned that's all. My word! Again, with the PMSing!"

"Well, just don't start with me again. I'll tell you what you want to hear, when I'm ready, but just don't push me!"

Etta Mae walked over to look out the window. The stressful dialog between the two was beginning to take its toll.

"Ummph, that's strange, Josh's car is gone. Wonder where he and Tonika went."

"Don't get me wrong." Dee said, addressing their earlier conversation.

"I knew he was a little too young, but Damien *is* a looker, which is probably what attracted me to him in the first place."

"Wait! You say he was young?"

Etta Mae turned with a puzzled look on her face.

"You into making headline news now like those cradle robbing school teachers?"

"Ha, ha! Aren't you funny? Let's just say, I've had them old and now I've had them young. So there, what's it to 'ya?"

"Oh, it's nothing to me, sister. That is, just as long as no cradles were robbed while you were *having them young.* You'll free to do whatever tickles your fancy."

"Well, thank you mother, for your permission." Dee said, curtseying in jest.

"I should've known something was up with you. It's not as if we were invited to your quickie wedding."

"No time to waste. It was a whirlwind romance and before I knew it, I was Mrs. Damien Whitman."

"And just like that you became Mrs. Delilah Carol Collins Melvin Cox Jefferson Whitman.

Oh wait, I forgot one; Simmons! I can't leave him out." Etta Mae said breathlessly.

"Stop being so mean, would you!" Dee said in her defense. "I'm just doing what's done in society, especially by men. But no one talks about how many times they marry. Now do they?"

"Now Delilah…" Etta Mae cautioned.

"Besides, I'm not the first, and I certainly won't be the last. What's good for the goose is certainly good for the gander!"

"No! That's not true… And I wouldn't go throwing any morals away, just because the world says it okay."

"Are you forever preaching? Geez!"

"No, but I'm just saying the ways of the world will have you going to hell with a coat on. After all, the world *is* the system of Satan you know."

Dee chuckled at her sister's sanctimonious view on life.

"Honey, let me tell you this one thing… Miss Delilah lives her life the way Miss *De-lilah* designs to live it. And besides, I couldn't stand to part with my luxurious mink coat anyway. Say… you sure you won't join us heathens?"

"Delilah Carol! Don't you play with me like that!"

Etta Mae made a swipe with her hand in her sister's direction.

"I won't be in that basket with you bunch of …"

"Are you sure?"

"*Listen*, when that sweet chariot swing low … honey; its surely going 'a let *me* ride."

Etta Mae lifted her eyes and hands to heaven.'Cause, I surely got a home on the other side."

"Well, ride on King Jesus!" The defiant one playfully said.

"Be careful now you're on the verge of blasphemy."

"Sorry Sis, you're right, but even you know there're plenty of women who're looking to the fountain of youth when it comes to their men."

"Cougars, I believe they are calling them now." Etta Mae said in agreement.

"I know what they're called. I'm not that much out of it that I don't know the haps!"

"Well, you do think too much inside the box when it comes to life in general. But I suppose that comes from your upbringing!" Etta Mae said.

"I know you've got to be careful out there, because the world is certainly different than it was when we were growing up. Of course, I could be wrong, so don't quote me on it."

"Oh, you don't have to worry about that, it's not something I care to repeat."

"I'm sure you wouldn't, but look 'a here, even in biblical times, they had to fend off 'ole slew foot.' So why do you think today would be any different?"

"I never said it was." Dee said, preparing herself for another of her sister's biblical renditions. And Etta Mae didn't disappoint.

"Girl, let me tell you. There was this woman in the scriptures that had seven demons...."

"Okay, okay, stop right there. I don't want to hear about some possessed woman way back when."

"Now you see that's the problem. You think the Scriptures were written just to collect dust?"

"I don't know, but I'm sure you 're about to tell me." Dee said cupping her head in both hands.

"Somebody rescue me... Please!"

CHAPTER

Just the thought of something like contracting the HIV virus was too farfetched for the relieved man. The counseling/testing center had been very adamant about the perils of practicing unsafe sex. He'd finally realized the danger he'd put himself in, not to mention his wife.

Damien Whitman was thankful 'mother luck' had been on his side as his fingers closed around the apartment keys.

He'd returned to the home he shared with his socialite wife, after a rough night alone at a nearby hotel. He'd left after the confrontation with his wife. There was no reasoning with her at the time.

The lock clicked as he turned the key. The heavy metal door easily swung open after a forceful push. He entered not knowing what to expect.

He hoped by now his wife was ready to discuss the issue in a more civilized manner.

The apartment was empty. Damien rushed into the luxurious gold and white embossed paneled bedroom. There, all he found were opened dresser drawers and closets, the evidence of hurried packing.

He stood in the center of the room and dropped to his knees. His body was racked with great gulping sobs.

Damien hadn't meant for his mere curiosity to go that far.

He'd meant to end the impromptu encounters months ago.

"Just this last time and no more, I swear." He had mentally promised himself.

The whole fiasco had all started with that one chance encounter on a rainy day.

Keith Easton a deceptively manly man, tall, dark, and handsome had been an Account Executive on Wall Street.

Coincidentally, he and Damien had met while hailing a cab on a busy New York Street.

Drenched in a down pour, they'd both reached for the cab's handle simultaneously. Damien was willing to forego his claim and offered to catch another one as so did Keith.

"Oh, I'm sorry this one is yours, I'll catch another." Damien had offered.

"No you take it." Keith had retorted.

A young lady standing a few feet away had watched the scenario being played out.

She had suddenly whisked past the two gentlemen; opened the car door; settled in the back seat and had directed the driver "Twenty-fifth and Broadway." And away the cab went.

The two perplexed gentlemen had been left standing in the rain.

The two had sought refuge in a nearby bar while waiting the end of the downpour, and had struck up a progressive conversation.

They had hoped to be able to savage what was left of their now possibly ruined Italian suits.

Formal introductions had been made. Likes and dislikes had been discussed.

Finally, marital status became the topic of interest. Keith it seemed had never married and had shared with Damien that he was gay. Strangely enough, Damien was taken aback by the well dressed bank executive's declaration.

He had coughed as his third vodka and martini had found its way down the wrong pipe.

Keith had reached over and had given his back a few whacks.

"You alright partner!"

Keith had allowed his hand to linger and had begun a slow circular rub on Damien's back.

Their eyes had met. Keith had already sensed the questions forming in the nervous gaze that stared back at him.

He'd seen that look before; "curious, but not bold enough to venture into unchartered terrain." His hand had kept up the steady motion.

The distraction of the constant rubbing had caused confusing thoughts in Damien's brain.

Confused by the unwelcomed feelings, he'd reached to remove the surprisingly soft, manicured hand only to have it covered instead by conjurer's other hand.

"I-I'm okay, uh, hmm, sorry."

Damien had stammered as he took another gulp from his glass.

The stealthy conjurer had leaned in for a presumably long kiss. Damien had pulled back at first and had lowered his head.

Keith, not one to be dissuaded by the man's shyness, had brought his face closer and the two had openly kissed.

They had talked long afterwards. Keith had emphasized that even married men were prone to walk on the 'wild side' every once in awhile.

It was at this point that the two gentlemen had decided to take their mere encounter a little further.

Going out into the sunny evening they had arrived at Keith's swank apartment.

The tryst had ended almost as soon as it had begun. After getting to know Keith more intimately, Damien had decidedly found that he hadn't cared for the promiscuous lifestyle of his initiating partner.

But the one sure thing that had come out of the chance relationship was the homosexual tendencies that had once lain dormant in the 'man on man' novice had now been awakened.

He had discreetly begun pursuing the newly discovered desires, all while carefully playing the role of a doting husband to an unsuspecting Delilah.

Damien Darnell Whitman began life as an only son in a small Georgia town, as a preacher's kid.

He had grown up hearing the Word, night and day, day and night.

It would be hard pressed for anyone to understand what he'd endured and surprisingly enjoyed while growing up.

He vividly recalled the many late nights spent with his heavy head with spittle drooling from his lips, straining to stay awake during his father's many late night services.

The 'Tabernacle of the Congregation Holiness Church'in a little town in Georgia, hosted a small congregation composed of mostly matronly mothers.

Very few of his school aged peers occupied the burgundy.

The wooden benches hadn't exactly been the soft padded cushions well-defined derrières sat on today.

His father's office was situated inside the church's parsonage, located next door.

Damien could often hear Pastor J.J. Whitman discussing private matters with his parishioners.

He'd learned not to ask any questions about anything he'd overheard or whose problems were being discussed.

The naive youngster had once made the mistake of inquiring, only to receive a serious paddling from his father, who had insisted on his confidentiality.

The years had flown by and like the dutiful son he was, the well-disciplined lad had remained faithful to his parents and that little church.

If there was anything he could pinpoint in his life that may've caused him to be in the predicament he now faced, was when an unforeseen incident happened in the church basement.

A staunch and respected male member of his father's congregation had forcibly raped him in one of the men toilet stalls when he was just thirteen years old.

The violated lad had then been threateningly warned never to divulge the incident to anyone. Which he never did. Damien had silently relived the horror for many years. Apparently, from the looks of things, it was then the 'seed of perversion' had been planted.

Years later both his parents had passed away while he was in college. His father first and then a year later his mother.

After the funerals Damien never returned to the little church or to his hometown.

Fortunately, after attending the historically black college in Georgia, he had landed a job as a Hedge Fund Banker in the financial district of New York City.

The extremely profitable source of income him to live a profitable life and was more than he could've hoped for. A substantial savings account was the result of hard work.

Not long afterwards Delilah, a popular recently divorced socialite soon came into his life. She frequented the inner financial circles of the high class society.

He knew her to be ten years his senior. The age difference had done little to dim the now captivated suitor's interest in the 'designer clad' vixen. Besides, in today's society, he'd reasoned, age was nothing but a number.

Delilah had joined the ever growing number of older women who found dating younger men more pleasurable than dating men their own age or older.

The courtship had begun and had eventually led to marriage.

Damien suppressed the thought that perhaps subconsciously, he had sought a mother figure more so than a wife in the May- December relationship.

The distraught husband sat in the middle of the floor. His mind refocused on the plight he now faced.

Delilah had walked in on him and his latest conquest in her mahogany four poster bed.

Dumbfounded, she had let out a blood curdling scream.

Damien had been so sure his languishing bride would be taking the usual full four hours at her weekly 10:00 spa that he'd somehow gotten careless.

But a throbbing ingrown toenail on her right foot had prompted an earlier than usual return home.

The effeminate young man had just been a pick-up at the same high-end bar he and Keith had met.

"How could you!" She had screamed, bursting into tears. *"Damn it to hell!* How could you!"

The agonizing look on her face would forever be branded in his memory.

"I have to go after her!" Damien decidedly declared.

Even though the short flight to New Jersey would give little time to think of what he would say or do Damien grabbed his medium size Carrington Luggage and threw in a few items of clothing and toiletries.

Worried thoughts of the uncertainty of the future were running a muck while riding the elevator down of his future gave way to a sense of urgency.

He hailed a yellow cab and jumped into the backseat.

Delilah had shared many stories with him of her childhood.

He knew how much her big sister meant to his wife.

"To LaGuardia please! He shouted to the turban wearing Indian driver.

Damien made a phone call while en route to the airport.

CHAPTER
Seven

....

E tta Mae poured herself another cup of hot brew. She turned to the window and saw her neighbor drag a trash can to the curb.

"Mm mm, I wonder what's up, wonder why she's putting the trash out and not Josh."

She had not realized she had spoken aloud.

"Something's happening over there… and I still don't see Josh's car."

The defiant sibling felt guilty about her earlier harsh reply and came up behind Etta Mae fully intending to offer an apology.

The moment of bonding was stolen as her eyes followed her sister's gaze.

"Oh, I see your best bud is coming over… I'll be in my room."

"Yes, that's Tonika, you remember her, don't you?"

Dee gave Etta Mae's shoulder a reassuring touch, and retreated down the hall. The last thing she wanted was to be drawn into any gossip.

Tonika lightly tapped the doorbell before letting herself in. The friends exchanged hugs. Etta Mae sat her cooled brew down, and replenished it with more hot liquid.

"Hey, neighbor! What're you up to on this fine Saturday morning?"

"Oh, about 5' 7" and a 130 lbs." The witty neighbor helped herself to a cup of coffee.

"I just took out the trash so I thought I'd stop over to see what was up with you."

She glanced around making sure they were alone. She hadn't wanted to share her marital woes in front of Etta Mae's sister.

"I see the old 'broomstick' has left for the green already."

"Yep, now you know he's at his usual place."

Etta Mae raised the cup to her lips, but lowered it, deciding instead to address the elephant in the room.

"Please tell me why you were messing with the trash. Where's Josh?"

Tonika's head slowly dropped as she sat in silence and stared into her cup. Words just could not seem to make their way past the lump forming in her throat.

"My sister Dee is here somewhere; if she comes out of her room, maybe you'll get a chance to meet her." Etta Mae offered sensing her friend's discomfort of the subject.

The understanding matron reached over and patted her hurting friend's arm.

"And girl, you know you don't need any excuse to come over here."

Tonika covered Etta Mae's hand with her own and squeezed it gently.

"Dee… came in from New York yesterday?"

"Yep, I picked her up at the airport at exactly 12:20."

"Ooh, I remember, yes, she's a stickler for time. When she was here last…"

"She may be, but it doesn't matter to me."

"Sounds like you weren't expecting her."

"I wasn't, but she's welcome anytime she wants to pop in. You never know with Miss Dee."

"It must be nice." Tonika said. "Everybody ain't got it like that."

"Ah girl, she's just going through something right now. I'm just glad I can be here for her."

"Do you know what she's going through?" Tonika asked, stirring sugar in her coffee. "Having problems with hubby maybe?"

"Couldn't tell you something I don't know. And if she knew I was discussing her *business*…Well, let me just tell you; Hell hath no fury!"

"Miss Etta…you're always there for everyone…even me."

"Whoa, where did that come from? What's up Toni? You're acting like your world just ended."

Etta Mae gave her amigo's hand a reassuring squeeze once again.

"I'm here darling, I'm here." Now she grasped both hands.

"I just don't know what…"

Donnie came in from the garage at that moment with his golf clubs. He left them to stand in the middle of the kitchen floor.

Tonika hurriedly wiped her face with her sleeve, and sipped her coffee.

"Whew! I'm glad to be out of all that humidity."

He soon realized he'd walked in at an inopportune moment after he noticed what looked like tears on his neighbor's face.

"Sorry for barging in, but it looks like you two had a pity party going on. Tonika, girl did your cat die or something?"

"Honey… now have a heart. I don't think your friend is up to your usual antics this morning."

Then Etta Mae turned her attention to the discarded golf bag.

"And are you going to leave that golf bag right there?"

"Ya' think!"

Donnie opened the refrigerator and took out a cold beer.

"Sweetie, I know you're proud of your bag and all…and it is quite exquisite, but your boys don't belong in the middle of my kitchen."

"Yeah, yeah, I'll move 'em in a minute."

He took a long swallow from the cold thirst quenching brew. He touched the cold can to his sweat moistened forehead.

"I just need to practice my putting skills. Why…are they bothering you or something? How's Ashad, Tomika?"

"He's doing fine, thanks for asking." She said in a barely audible voice. "The Johnsons are picking him up for practice in a few hours."

"Oh, that's good. So he plays soccer with Brenda and Hank's grandkids?"

"Yes, he and Jared are good friends."

"And the answer is no, to your question, honey." Etta Mae interjected.

"They're not bothering me, but still, I don't want to trip over them later. You know how forgetful you can be."

61

"I can see the old girl's not herself, but she'll bounce back in no time. Right, To-mi-ka?"

He gave his friend an old 'atta girl' nudge.

The concerned friend that he was, Donnie thought perhaps butchering her name would draw his saddened colleague out of her funk.

He wanted to create a much needed smile on her gloomy face.

"To-mi-ka, you drink all my coffee?"

Tonika realized that now wasn't a good time to bear her dirty laundry.

She composed herself and decided she may as well join in the friendly banter with her pesky neighbor.

"Donnie Leroy Smith! Would you get hooked on phonics? My name *is* ... Tonika! With an 'n,' thank you very much."

"Tonika, Tomika, Chaquita, whatever!"

Donnie gave his wife a quick kiss on the cheek before taking another sip of beer.

"Lord, you sure are pouring it on a little strong." Donnie responded to her remark by distorting his face.

"Anyway, baby...What's for dinner?

"Hey, Sweet Daddy!" Etta Mae winked at Tonika.

"I'm glad you're back, I missed you this morning, not unlike any *other* Saturday morning."

"To-*mi*-ka, your lights get cut off again, the reason you're here?" Donnie inquired, ignoring Etta Mae's slight.

"No! And Etta Mae took your grocery money... and paid my bill. So there!"

"Now... *honey!*"

Donnie was pleased with Tonika's reaction to his wordplay, and took it a little further.

"Darn it, I know you didn't spend any of my hard earned money on 'Miss Thang' here!

Not when there're candles in the kitchen that ole 'Miss Down-On-Her-Luck,' could've had."

"Donnie, you know I take great care of your money!"

The ladies feet made contact under the counter.

"Um humph, I know your ole' bleeding heart… Everybody's a neighbor self." Donnie quipped.

"What money?"

Tonika asked while she pushed harder against her friend's foot.

"You sure you didn't get your pink slip yesterday? You're on that damn golf course too much for anyone to be working!"

Laugher filled the cozy kitchen. Tonika felt much better, now that she was able to laugh.

She was grateful to her best friends for having lifted her spirit.

"With all those budget cuts going on…Etta, girl if I were you I'd call his job on Monday."

"*Excuse you!* I don't recall sleeping in your bed! And why are you so concerned about my job? Last time I checked my pay stub, it read Donnie L. Smith!"

"And… I believe I have a blessing on the way."

Tonika rubbed her thumb against her fingers. Then she pointed to Donnie. "And I'm looking at 'im!"

"Humph, Negro, please; you wish." Donnie slapped at Tonika's hand.

"Donnie, my dear friend; you're supposed to "love your neighbor as you love yourself."

Now that's Scripture, am I right girl-friend?"

"Now, Toni, I'm no fool… I love you, but we ain't exactly got it like that!"

She grabbed her man around his waist.

"I can't be wasting my Boo's hard earned cash."

"*Ha!* Now you talking baby. It's good to hear my money is in good hands!"

Donnie playfully pulled away from his wife's grasp and bent down to be eye level with his neighbor.

"And for your information 'Miss All-Up-In-My-*Busi-ness*' … I just happened to have gotten a raise just this week, thank you very much."

This time he directed his attention to Etta Mae.

"Babe we're in the money! No budget cuts here, no sir-ee."

"O, Boo! Why didn't you tell me?"

His wife playfully whined. She grabbed her husband's waist once again.

"Tonika, gir-rrl… we're going shopping."

"Oh, no you're not! Not on my money, you're not. That's exactly why I didn't tell your old butt in the first place!"

He unclasped his wife's hands and stepped away.

"I tell you, a man always has to keep an ace in the hole to get ahead!"

"But *Hon-ey*… Etta Mae said with pouted lips. "You've been holding out on me… O' Boo, I'm crushed."

"Don't but honey me, a man has to draw the line somewhere, especially when it comes to his pockets."

The conversation is interrupted by the ringing of the phone. Donnie went over to answer it.

"Hello? Who is this? ... Who?"

He turned to give to give his wife a puzzled look.

"Yes, this is the Smith's residence…. Is … excuse me! Who's gone?

Now look here, before I answer any of your questions, I think you'd best answer mine. So, who may I say is calling?"

Donnie heard a click at the other end of the line.

"Damn! The fool hung up!"

"He hung *up*…was it Damien?" Etta Mae asked. "He didn't want to talk to his wife?"

"The fool didn't say who he was, and I didn't know him from *Adam*!"

Needless to say, Donnie was a little miffed over the whole conversation.

"Well, I can see he got under your collar." Etta Mae said.

"You're darn right! I sure wasn't about to give out any answers unless he'd answered mine." He took another long swig of his beer. "Now, would you?"

"Well you should've known who it was." Etta Mae said defensively. "No one else would be calling for … at least, I don't think."

"Who can keep up with the men in your sister's life?" Donnie shouted back.

"It's not like we've ever met him. Although… I did hear him say, something about he didn't even know she was gone, before he abruptly hung up."

The phone call only made the fidgety mother-hen more anxious to get to the bottom of her sister's situation.

Tonika, concluded the sorrows of her life would need to be put on hold. From the sound of it, a more pressing issue was at stake in this household.

Donnie fished a ball out of his pant pocket and grabbed a putting iron from the free-standing golf bag. One of Etta Mae's beige and blue floral patterned Pfalzgraff coffee mug served as a makeshift receptacle.

"Whatever was going on between his sister-in-law and her husband was none of his business." He'd reasoned.

But, true to form, all his calculated efforts proved futile as the ball by-passed the cup and rolled all the way into the dining room.

Donnie's second attempt was no better than the first. This time the ball sideswiped the cup and rolled under the credenza.

"*What's* your problem today?" He shouted.

"Well, Donnie." Tonika jokingly said. "That's no surprise. We can't exactly call you 'Mr. T. Woods' now can we?"

Donnie turned his back to her taunting humor. As for Tonika, she had just gotten started and wouldn't let up.

"If you ask me, I'd say you're more like a Tigger." The women shared a laugh. "Now where did you abandon Winnie?"

"Woman, I don't know what you're talking about. I may not be the 'Tiger,' but I am his big brotha!"

"You wish." Tonika countered. "Last I heard his Momma only had one son."

The little white ball's refusal to go into the cup had Donnie's nerves on end. Thanks to his neighbor's constant chatter, his concentration was off.

"And why should today be any different?" Tonika said, smirking. "Let's just say, the only green blazer you'll be wearing is the one you buy."

"Oh, Lord, I pray it's not a green one." Etta Mae added, still a bit puzzled over the phone call.

"He won't be going anywhere with me in a green blazer!"

"Forget you! Tonika"

Donnie had become increasingly agitated with the two women for doubting his golfing skills.

"It's not as if I'm trying to get a Ryder's Cup, damn it! Etta Mae you'd better get your girl; before I knock—

"Before you do what?" Tonika jumped up with blazon fists. "And I suppose you haven't met Bert and Ernie here."

"*Ha, ha, ha!* Sit down girl; now you two behave."

Etta Mae playfully stood between the two warring parties and jokingly slapped her friend on the arm.

"Do I have to get my strap?"

"Your strap?" Tonika asked. "Oo! Etta Mae, you have a strap?" She found Etta Mae's threat humorous. "It wouldn't be a two prong whip, now would it?"

"Ooh, that's so kinky! You two old coots—

"Uh, slow your road Miss Freak-a-zoid." Etta Mae interjected. "And get your mind out of the gutter…. We ain't down like that; huh Boo?"

Donnie was oblivious to the garish humor.

"Nope, my man Tigue don't have to worry about me taking any of his trophies."

Then as in afterthought, he turned his attention back to the women.

"Say, didn't I ask about dinner earlier? Well, what're we having, wife of mine?"

"Yes, wifey, what exactly are we having?" Tonika mimicked.

"*We?* Since when do we include Donnie, Etta Mae and To-mika?" Donnie jokingly blasted.

"You won't be parking those size tens under my table tonight." They all laughed.

"Surprise yourself, honey, and make me and my friend here dinner too while you're at it."

"Yes 'Tig,' a nice juicy steak would go good right about now. And I want mine raa-re." Tonika mimicked a tiger's roar. "*Roa-aaaar!*"

"Here Cha-*mi*ka." Donnie made a fist at Tonika. "Here! I got your rare steak, but it won't be as rare as your lip!"

Tonika returned the gesture. She got up to replenish her cup.

"Is your husband working yet?"

Donnie sent a blaze of light hearted questions her way.

"What kind of work does he do? Where is he anyway? Shouldn't you be with him?"

"Now, be nice, honey!"

Etta Mae quickly intervened, in an attempt to salvage her bosom buddy's emotions. She understood her unsuspecting companion was up to his jovial antics once again.

"*An-nd*...once again *butthead!* My name is To-*ni*-ka! And my husband is an entrepreneur. He's just in between projects at the moment. Thank you very much."

Oh, so now Josh's job is...." Donnie imitated washing a phantom windshield. "Hello sir, mind if I wash your windshield? Ah, that'll be two dollars, please."

He jumped backwards from the imaginary car and yelled. "Hey! Watch the toes!"

"Honee. You're so bad. Please leave Tonisha alone. Oops! I meant To-ni-ka! Sorry, friend."

The husband and wife slapped hi-fives.

The benignant neighbor couldn't help but laugh despite herself. This was the reason she so enjoyed coming over to visit her friends.

If you were ever in a funky mood, it wouldn't last long around these two.

"Tonika, girl don't pay that class clown any mind, he's just being silly."

"*Him*...what about you? You're getting just as bad, but you know what? You two numbskulls are not going to worry me."

The house guest defiantly crossed her legs, and turned sideways in her seat.

"That's good, because you know we're just jiving." Etta Mae said. "Besides girl, we women have our ways when it comes to men anyway. Don't we?"

"At least some of us seem to." Tonika said distractedly.

"Oh my, I wasn't expecting that remark. I must say, you're acting a bit strange today. There wouldn't be anything specifically you wanted to tell me, would there?"

Tonika looked from Donnie then to Etta Mae. She finally decided to lay her soul bare.

"What the heck." She thought, "I'm sure they've already figured it out."

"Only that Josh is gone."

"Oh, no!" Etta Mae exclaimed.

Yep, I'm afraid so… He left yesterday, returned late last night and slept on the couch."

The distraught woman's tears flowed freely once again. Etta Mae went over to where she sat and gave her a tight squeeze.

"Where'd he go?" She asked.

"That, I couldn't tell you. All I know is he left this morning after packing most of his belongings."

"*So,* that's what he was doing when I saw him?"

Donnie said, as he watched the scene before him. He went over to the two consoling women.

"You mean my boy Josh has flown the coop? Like out of here? See 'ya! … I can't believe it!"

"Oh, stop with the questions already!" Tonika said, with bullets for eyes. She was not the least bit amused.

"Just let it go, I don't want to talk about it!"

"Tonika, girl, you have my permission to slap him!" Etta Mae said.

"And it's okay if you don't want to talk about it. I solely understand."

Etta Mae now becoming irritated at her husband's lack of sensitivity, silently mouthed for him to keep quiet.

"Thanks, I really appreciate you. And there's nothing funny about it, broomstick!" Tonika kicked at the snickering menace.

"Sure ain't!" Donnie said. "Not in the least bit." Then he thought to add. "Imagine that… No wonder the dude—

"Oh, would you just let it go!"

"Uh-oh, it's getting hot in here!" Donnie wittingly said. He wiped his forehead with the back of his hand.

"Oh, but for God sake, don't take off any of your clothes."

Determined to lighten the depressing atmosphere in the room, Donnie let out a nervous laugh.

However, the discomposed house guest's countenance remained downtrodden. From the looks on the women faces, he soon realized his jovial teasing was not welcomed.

Even Etta Mae was taken aback. He could sense the sorrow Tonika was feeling, but the only way he knew to help was to keep her laughing.

"Laughter does a heart merry. At least that's what it says in Proverbs 15:13. "A merry heart makes a cheerful countenance."

"Ooo... honey, I'm scared of you." The proud wife said to her Bible knowledge partner.

Basking in his newfound glory. Bobby McFerrin's song, *Don't Worry, Be Happy* comes to the forefront of his mind.

This was Donnie's outlook on life. He had found refuge under the shelter of laughter from a number of the 'enemy's storms.

The lone male figure in the room didn't honestly believe Josh would up and abandon his own family.

No real man would do that. In any case, it appeared his world and Josh's world was totally different.

The air was filled with silence, as they each sat lost in thought.

Etta Mae was the first to break the silence by initiating her amore into a conversation she knew was sure to lighten the mood.

"Hey, Boo... You know us gals have our way when it comes to you men. Don't we girl friend?"

"Huh... what're you talking about?" Tonika asked.

Do you think that's how Eve got Adam to bite that apple?"

"I don't know... It could be. You know what head men think with."

"Oh, here we go. Now you two instigators are messing with my man Adam." Donnie shouted. He pushed his golf gear into the living room, against a wall.

"What's my man done to you two?"

"Yep, my friend, you guessed it. All men are fair game, even your boy, Adam."

"Any-ways, that's my cue to exit, 'cause it sounds like man bashing time. So, I'm going 'a make like ya' friend's old-man and disappear. Now if you two ladies will excuse me."

Smiles and winks were directed at each other, by the two ladies, who were now satisfied they had succeeded in their plan.

"Whew-ee! I better hit the shower too." Donnie said lifting his shirt and sniffing his underarms.

"I need a shower, I'm all sweaty. I sure worked up a sweat pounding my clubs on the ground today."

"Pee-yew! Tonika readily added. "Yes you do, and do it quickly!"

As the offensive being with underarms exposed goes over to the Tonika and Etta Mae who uses their hands to fan their faces.

"Get away… Tonika said, pushing the pest away. "I thought I smelled a musk ox marking his territory."

"No … what you smelled is the scent of a man in his own home!" Donnie countered. "Is it enough to drive you away?"

"And did you happen to win 'Last Comic Bombing?'"

"Okay, you two. Quit it and go take your shower! Honey, ple-ee-aze!

"Oka-ay, already. Sheesh! Women folk! A fellow can't even go au natural in his own home."

Donnie pecked his wife on the cheek on his way out of the room.

"See ya' in a little bit, babe...Then we'll discuss what's for dinner. Tomika you won't be here when I get back will ya?"

"I surely hope that wasn't your last wish, my brother."

"Oh, honey, be sure to let my sister know she had a phone call."

Etta Mae proceeded over to the refrigerator.

"Tonika, do you want something else to drink besides that cold coffee?"

"Sure! I could go for a nice, cold one."

Donnie lifted the sweaty shirt over his head, as he walked down the hallway.

He stopped in front of the guestroom and gently knocked on the door. "Hello… Dee?"

"Come in." Dee said, awakening out of a fitful nap.

Donnie opened the door just a crack.

"Oh! I'm sorry. I didn't know you were napping. Donnie apologetically stated. "But I wanted to let you know your hubby called for 'ya earlier. That is, I guess it was hubby."

"What! Damien called here. And why did you say you guess? Either he did, or he didn't."

"Just calm down… all I know is that the phone rang; I answered it, but the caller didn't say who he was.

He just asked if you were here. So, I-I mean that is, your sister naturally assumed it was your husband."

"Oh, that man has some balls calling me!" Dee fumed.

"Why shouldn't he call you? Wait a minute… Do you mean you didn't let your husband know where you were going?"

Donnie throwing the reeking shirt around his neck stepped fully into the room.

"You care to tell me what's going on?"

An exaggerated sigh escaped her lips as she sat up smoothing the strands of hair that had dislodged from her up-do.

"Oh, Brother-law, how do I begin? More importantly, where do I begin?"

"How about starting from the beginning?" He said sitting on the edge of the bed. "Do you want to talk? I got time."

As Donnie sat down, Dee caught a whiff of his underarms and thought to herself.

I'll sure have to make this quick, so I don't prolong my boy's shower.

She reclined as far back as possible and began telling her woes.

CHAPTER

"Uh umm." Etta Mae cleared her throat at Tonika's beer request. "I was thinking more like lemonade, or a soda, Missy."

The "life has thrown you a lemon" recipient really wanted, and desperately needed a cold brew, but was willing to accept the lemonade.

"Well…Okay, nice cold *lemonade* then, but a beer sounds more refreshing!"

"I bet it does." Etta Mae resolving to give her hurting friend the beer she so desperately craved peered into the refrigerator only to find her thirsty spouse had taken the last one.

"Oops, sorry my friend, but my hubby took the last one. And it looks like we're all out of lemonade too! Darn! But I know you drink cola, so here.

"Girlie, you know me so well."

"And don't I know it, besides that's all there is. I truly must go grocery shopping *soon!*" Etta muttered handing her friend a can of cola.

"Thanks." Tonika took a long sip, hoping the cold sweet liquid would sooth her parched throat.

Just then her cell phone buzzed, she picked it up and read a text message.

"Oh, that's Ashad saying he was about to leave."

"Oh…How's my sweet boy?" Etta Mae asked. "Toni, you've done such a good job raising him."

"Thanks… but I couldn't have done it without you two. You were my life saver."

"You're welcome. And it was our pleasure." Etta Mae said. "Especially, since it doesn't look as if we'll be grandparents anytime soon."

"Oh, don't fret, my friend, maybe you'll get that call one day soon from Janet."

"One can only hope; but I was emphatically told by my beautiful daughter that she and Geoffrey wanted to enjoy each other for a while, before they started a family. Not to mention, enjoy Hawaii as well!"

"I can understand that."

"You know girlfriend, we mentioned my girl Eve earlier. Etta Mae said after they'd sat quietly for a moment.

"There has to be something to that you know."

"Um." Tonika sounded swallowing the sip of cola. "To be truthful, I hadn't honestly given it much thought. But where're you going with this?"

"Oh, it's just that I'd say the 'old girl' had put one over on us. Don't you think?"

"Oh… I see what you mean. I-I guess."

"Think about it Toni! She must have been something to make her man go against 'El Shaddai!'"

"Humph, well if you ask me, it wouldn't be too nifty for her sorry butt to be around here at this point and time." Tonika made a mock noose with her hands.

"A lot of women would just love to get their hands around that old neck of hers!"

"Boo!" Out of nowhere, an incarnated apparition appeared in the room.

The women were frightened beyond belief. They both jumped up clutching each other tightly.

"Whoa-a! Etta, who's t-that?" Tonika trembled in fear.

"Well…" Etta Mae reasoned. She began to offer the shaken woman the only explanation she knew.

"I k-know it's not Wilma Flintstone, so it's has to be Eve!"

"W-Why do you say th-that, E-Etta?"

"Who else would walk around in animal skin in this type of weather?"

Etta Mae looked toward the manifested figure with apprehension. Etta concluded her morning's vision apparently did open a portal into the spirit realm. But, for some strange reason her fear had begun to dissipate.

"Maybe, just maybe, this strange figure had been sent to deliver a message."

"Hold it together ladies. Fear not! For I bring you great tidings!" Eve offered an exhilarating greeting. She actually found the two women somewhat amusing.

"I believe that's how the angels say it when they pop in for a visit."

"Great tidings?" Tonika finally found the courage to ask. "From where; from what; and *who* exactly are you?"

"Tonika, I told you—

"Why I'm Eve And exactly where do you think I'm from? To-mi-ka! The apparition swaggeringly answered.

The startled woman's eyes widened at the brazen liberty taken with her name. Eve, on the other hand simply went on to say:

"I heard you two discussing me, so I thought I might pay you a little visit. You know... I decided it was time to tell my side of the story."

"Wait a minute!" Etta Mae shouted. "You said you heard us discussing you, how and what exactly did you hear?"

"I obviously heard enough to make me want to pop in on you two."

"Oh, and who knew it would bring about all this."

"Etta Mae... darling! I'm surprised at you. Have you forgotten Hebrews 12:1 you read this morning? "Therefore, we're surrounded by such a great cloud of witnesses...."

"You mean you were the one that caused me to turn to that passage."

"Well...let's just say ... as a cloudy witness..."

"You do have to know, however, that we're not exactly in the habit of talking to ghosts!" Tonika retorted. "It just ain't natural!"

"I wouldn't go so far as to say that."

"And my name by the way is with an 'N,' *To-ni-ka!*"

The irritated neighbor adamantly pointed out to the smirking phantom.

"No…It-'ain't'-natural." Eve mockingly said. *"But, like Etta Mae said this morning. "God is doing a new thing."*

"And just exactly what new thing is God doing?" Tonika wanted to know.

"Well… For one thing, He's simply putting the super on your natural. And, ladies, I'm not talking hair."

Eve tugged at her crown of natural locks.

"Get it…natural?"

She laughed at her own play on words, only to be met with blank stares.

"Besides, you guys are talking to ghosts nowadays like it's no big deal." Eve added. *"What's that box you all call t-tele-vision?"*

Yes, a television… tell-a-vision." Etta Mae interpreted.

"Okay, that thing! You can almost always find some undaunted hero going into a haunted house. "Speak to me, if you're in here."

"Yeah, yeah, and your point is?" Tonika said to Eve. "We know what you're implying; it's not as if we're dumb, you know."

Eve standing her ground with the arrogant human now placing both hands on her hips, emphatically states.

"Missy, the dumb thing about it all is that God showed you where He stood on all this in Deuteronomy 18:10;"Whoever practices witchcraft, sorcery, or who is a medium, a psychic or the like, is detestable to Him."

"And you said that to say what?" Tonika asked.

"That you hard headed humans, thinking you know everything… What do you do? You go and do just the opposite."

"It's all done in the name of science, thank you."

"Tell that to your Maker."

"Well, I won't bother Him, but now that you're here, it's my opportunity do what I said I'd do." Tonika said. She then stood and advanced toward the materialized specter.

"And that was to whip your butt!"

"Tonika! Girl, sit down!" Etta Mae demanded. "And calm down; it does not take all that!"

The quarrelsome damsel reluctantly returned to her seat. Satisfied that a crisis had been avoided, Etta Mae then said to Eve.

"So, girl friend, since you're here, we'll let you say your piece, because you have a lot of explaining to do—

"Woman, spirit, whatever you are!" Tonika shouted, before the specter could even speak.

"You don't have a side, all I know is, you blew it for all us women, and that's the bottom line!"

"Geez, could your pot boil any hotter?"

"What do you know about a boiling pot?" Etta Mae wanted to know. "You mean you had a pot to boil?"

Eve laughed, but watched the grouchy neighbor closely. She wasn't too concern with the animosity the distraught soul displayed toward her. Usually, that type often needed to vent their frustration at something, or on someone. So it may as well be against the *'Mother of all Living.'*

"Girl, uh, I meant Eve. Just tell us why you did what you did and what was the reason behind all of it?"

"What can I say? Other than, there was no excuse."

"My thoughts exactly!" Etta Mae said. "Honey, if anybody ever had it made, it had to be you!"

"And you don't think I know that all I had to do was just wander about that beautiful garden that our beautiful Creator provided for Adam and me."

Eve walked away from the women, absorbed in what she'd lost, but the moment of melancholy was interrupted.

"Yeah, she didn't even have to cook, clean, do laundry or anything.

That's probably why she got into trouble in the first place." Tonika ranted on.

"You know they say an "idol mind is the devil's workshop," and from the looks of it, her mind was pretty idol."

"Well, I wouldn't go so far as to say that, Miss Thang, but you're correct in one thing though."

"I am? And what might that be?"

"You were correct in the fact that all… I had to do was to pick a plant and eat it. Food, water, companionship… speaking of which, that was why I

was created you know, to be a companion to your boy Adam. I was supposed to be his help meet."

"And I would say you helped him meet alright, helped his butt right on out of that glorious garden!"

Etta Mae slapped a high-five with her neighbor. Eve rolled her eyes skyward and chose to ignore the women.

"After all, I am…bone of his bone, and flesh of his flesh. But no-o! Your girl messed up! I just had to go and wander off that day, being nosy.

Now, you know that's where you girls get that from …Me!"

"Now I know you're lying, I didn't get anything from you." Tonika said, defensively. "I'm not nosy! I'm, or we're merely observant. Now, am I right about it, girlfriend?"

"Yes, that's it. We're merely observant." Etta Mae said in agreement. "We observe this, and we observe that, and if that's not being nosy, then I don't know what is." She said, slapping her open palm on the table. "Now, would you just shush!"

"Yes, Toni, shush!"

Eve had wanted to say that to the annoying human herself and was overjoyed when the woman's cohort had done just that.

"Then that ole wily serpent appeared in that tree and got the best of me. He probably had been watching me the whole while!

Come telling me; "Sssssss… now you know God is withholding something from you and Adam. There is something he doesn't want you to know… Sssssssss."

Now you know my ears perked up, don't you?"

"Your *ears* perked up? Sweetie, you're referring to a talking snake! I know what Tonika would have perked up alright…My perked up association would have hauled butt out of there."

"Now, why would you run Miss Scaredy-Cat?" It was only a little ole snake."

"Well honey, around here snakes don't talk."

This time Etta Mae is the one to stand to her feet.

"I'm sure I do not have to tell you… if I ever ran up on a live snake, honey he would be one dead snake, because Mama *does-not-play-that!"*

The women laughed at Etta Mae's demonstration of stomping on a snake.

"Now I know you women aren't scared of a little old snake. Not when I see you wrapping them all around your neck and dance with them.

'Un, un, I ain't the one! You won't catch Sistah Girl dancing with a stupid snake!"

"But then look who I'm talking to, 'Miss Erie Etta' and her side kick, 'Miss Timid Toni."

"What did you call us?" Tonika asked, demanding to know. Rising to approach Eve once again.

"Etta Mae, you hear that? I know you're lying now! You haven't seen me wrapping no snake round this neck!"

"Oh, just hold your horses. Eve said, backing up. *"Did I say you? Well, I meant women in general. And do the both of you know you're supposed to put enmity between you and the serpent?"*

The ladies shook their heads in recognition.

Now please, allow me to continue."

"Good, but let's clarify; I'm not touching anybody's slimy snake! *Uuuugh!"* Tonika shuddered and sat down.

"Thank you, Miss 'G.' Now if you remember, little ole me was pulled from Adam's side, you know his rib. So I was a big part of the Man. You understand. The specter asked, looking expectantly. It's like this... I, Eve represents Adam's conscious side. That is his 'soul.'

"You what?" Etta Mae inquired. "His soul, you say?"

"I'm surprised at you, 'Bible-worm.' Yes, his soul. Your soul is your feelings, your thinker, your emotions, and your will power? And even still, your chooser? You didn't know that?"

"I know it now."

"Good! I'm glad you do, because old Satan knew it too. And he knew just who to come to. Me!"

"Yeah, and you lost your soul, and everyone else's, right then and there!" Tonika said.

"Hel-lo! Let's just say the snake piqued my curiosity. Okay Missy?

The ladies finally settled down and gave Eve the chance to tell a large chunk of her tale.

"Why, that lying piece of... Well, I don't have to spell it out for you, do I?"

"No, we can sort of garner what happened."

"He was hanging out in this beautiful tree loaded with delectable fruit. Needless to say, I bit into the fruit. But, do you know nothing happened. Though somehow, I knew I'd messed up.

Now, you know I couldn't be in this mess alone. If I were going down, Brother-Man was going down with me!

So, I put on my best womanly charm, and when Adam approached he couldn't resist. He bit too! And now both our eyes were opened. Right off, we both realized we were naked."

Eve seductively swayed her hips.

"Now, for the first time, Adam looked at me with lust in his eyes."

"Girl, quit jiving!" Tonika said with disbelief. "You mean to tell me, there you are standing there butt naked and your man never drank you in with his eyes? Come on now, Miss Evie."

"Hold up, Tonika, she could be right you know." Etta Mae said. "What does the Bible say about lust? That it was a sin, right? And because of what was done, she and Adam's eyes were now opened to that sin."

"Okay, I get it. They were innocent in their love for each other before then."

"Now, don't forget Miss Etta, we were husband and wife; so our lust wasn't a sin."

"You're so right, Eve girl! My bad." Etta Mae admitted.

"Apology accepted... Now I know many of you have often wondered why Adam also ate of the fruit."

Eve paced back and forth. She paused ever so often to drive home her point. Tonika and Etta Mae hung on to her every word.

"Ladies, you see Adam represented the 'spirit part of man. Remember, he was made in the image of God, who is Spirit and who is also the very embodiment of Love." Eve hugged herself before continuing.

"Now you see, because Adam was made in the image of God, and because Adam loved me, he chose not to separate from me, and leave his woman hanging or his soul per se.

So, my 'Boo' bit into that fruit, bringing us three back together again, body, soul and spirit. Otherwise, where would you two be?"

With the snap of her fingers the two women became more alert. Etta Mae and Tonika looked at each other and simply shrugged their shoulders.

"But, ladies, do you know what the drawback was?" Eve began to sob.

"The drawback of it all was that even though Adam and me were together… We were separated from our glorious Creator."

"Please don't cry." Etta Mae said. She extended her arms to offer comfort, but thought better of it and quickly pulled back.

"I'm sure you didn't… and by the way, it's Adam and I."

"Oh, so now we're suddenly into using proper English. So, what was up with your word 'ain't' being thrown around so freely?"

"Etta! What are you doing? You don't have to pity her. I bet she knew exactly what she was doing, all along!"

However, Etta Mae was convinced differently and seemingly had an epiphany moment.

"Tonika girl, it makes sense though! I never thought of it like that before. I've always wondered why Adam went against his *Creator*."

"I can't believe you fell for that cheap display of humility."

Eve watched the two ladies out of the corner of her eye. She fully realized the troubled neighbor was a force to be reckoned with.

"Wow! You see, you learned something new today!" Etta Mae grabbed hold of Tonika's arm. "And I hate to say it, but I'm glad she came."

"Well, if you ask me, there was no choice to be made."

Tonika used her hands as scales, in weighing her decision.

"Eve; God? God; Eve? Nope! No comparison!"

Eve flippantly addressed the clueless women.

"Okay, Miss Lady, here's a question for you. If you think the decision was that easy; then why don't more of you choose Him today?"

"What do you mean by that?" Etta Mae asked.

"Yes, why did you say that? You hear us crying all the time; God bless America! We are a Bible believing nation."

"Are you two serious, or just clueless? I believe you also have what you call your atheists and your agnostics in-this-nation as well."

Etta Mae lowered her head. She didn't need to be reminded of that very fact.

"Ummph, I have to admit girlfriend, you're so right."

They each pondered the question. Then Tonika made what she considered an amazing observation.

"But do you know what's funny about all that?"

"What?"

"That very same big group of 'A' list people share in the very same blessings we believers do in this nation. Do you see how good our God is?"

"You know it, because He rain on the just, as well as the unjust! And here's another one for 'you.'"

Eve was pleased with her ability of finally stomping the belligerent human.

"The sin wasn't brought about because of the fruit.... No...The sin came about from our disobedience.

The very fact that we took the 'serpent's word over His 'Word,' was what did it! So there you have it, so to speak, in a nutshell!"

"Now, I don't have an answer for you there." Etta Mae said. "All I can say is you two sure had some balls."

Tonika shook her head in agreement. Etta Mae's statement confused the non-human.

"Oh, you don't know about having balls?"

"What she means is; you two hard heads had some nerves … guts! You know, intestinal fortitude to go against 'the Almighty' like you did!"

Eve stood in silence, with her head bowed. No words were said between either of them for a long time.

CHAPTER
Nine

....

"Donnie." Dee said. "You're a man—I, uh, I mean a man's man. Right?" She stammered, suddenly feeling uncomfortable.

"Hell ye-ahh! Duhhh! Why? Why do you ask?"

"Oh, I'm sorry, I didn't mean for you to think I was questioning your manhood."

"Oh, I'm okay with it." Donnie said with a deeper voice than necessary.

"Well, it's just that I can't fathom why a man would want to look at another man."

"Good grief, so that's it! Don't tell me your husband is on the 'DL,' the 'Down Low!'"

The look on Dee's face answered for her silence.

"Oh my Lord, Delilah!"

"Yep, you got it."

"Da-amn! That's some deep shi—Uh, sorry." Donnie uttered apologetically. "My bad."

"Who're you telling? And the way I found out was… Well, I'm not ready to give details just yet. I'm still coming to grips with it." Donnie, understandably, didn't press for further details. He could sense how hard it must be for his sister-in-law.

"Oh, I understand, and believe me when I say I don't think I could stomach it anyhow. E-eww!" He shuddered at the thought.

"Thanks for understanding, because I wouldn't wish anything like what happened to me on my worst enemy."

"So what are you going to do?" Donnie asked with genuine concern. "I mean with your marriage and all?"

"I don't know. I told my sister I was divorcing, but truthfully, I honestly don't know.

I obviously love my husband, but I needed to get away, to clear my head."

"Well, you can stay here as long as you like. And your sister. what are you going to tell her?"

"I don't know … I feel so much like a failure, and I don't want her to worry about me."

"Have you told her anything besides you're getting a divorce?"

"No, I haven't, but I was about to this morning."

Dee raised her hand to signal a stop.

"Just believe me when I tell you, I dread the moment."

"I'm sure she's wondering—"

"I know; I know… so you don't have to tell me. Dang! I'm sure she is."

"Al-though, she's surprising me with just how patient she's being. It's out of her character not to push to get to the bottom of an issue."

"I know how she is, and then there's her gal pal!"

"What was that?"

"Now Dee, I have to come to my wife's defense. I'm sure she's just giving you time to sort through things. So don't let that hinder you from going to her… Promise?"

"Okay already, I promise. Geez!"

She reluctantly agreed then thoughtfully admitted.

"You're right, but this is just not something I want, or think I can talk to her about."

"I don't know why not."

"Bro-law, you know her righteous stance on everything." She searched his face for understanding. "You understand, don't you?"

"I admit it has got to be hard, but the ball is in your court."

"My sister would want to know every detail, and I'm not ready for that! Nobody knows the hell I'm going through right now!"

"Calm down, please. I tell you what… You sleep on it a little longer, and then we'll see."

He rose from the bed, but before he reached the door, he said to his sister-in-law.

"Say what you want, but my baby has a very big heart!"

"Yes, she does at that, and she always has." Dee said.

She smiled as she got up from the bed to give her dear brother-in-law a loving hug.

"Thanks for listening. Now go take your shower, please." They both laughed.

"You're certainly welcome, that's what families are for. When you hurt we hurt."

"Thank you, Bro-law."

You're welcome, but my advice to you is not to keep it from your sister too much longer. Okay, Delilah?"

"Oh my, Delilah again. Now that's some serious stuff. but I do promise."

Dee returned to the bed and closed her weary eyes.

"To-morrow."

"Good." Donnie said leaving the room.

CHAPTER

....

"I still say, everyone's responsible for their own decisions, as well as their own actions." Etta Mae said, seizing the reins once again. "The thing is our Father only wants those who come to Him, to come willingly."

Eve pondered the housewife's comment over in her mind knowing how deeply troubled the Creator had become behind she and Adam's disobedience.

"Yep, the Creator was deeply hurt. And I can tell you truthfully it still grieves His Spirit when one of his creations becomes eternally separated from Him."

With the revealing remarks now bringing tears to one captive listener, Etta Mae's next words is but a testimony to how much she was affected.

"You know what? She said through tears. "I don't know about you two, but if I had the power to save the world I would do it, just to make Him happy again."

"Ah...hel-lo-o!" Earth to Etta!" Tonika, said, directly addressing her friend. "Well duh! It's already been done. Remember?"

"Yes! I remember!" Etta snapped back.

Now feeling emboldened she'd somehow manage to stomp the 'Bible thumper' in her tracks, Tonika went on to say.

"Yes! Praise God. And His precious blood was shed for you and for me." Then turning to Eve, with newly found revelation went on to add. "Better still even for her; the one who started it all."

"Yes, girlfriend! Etta began. "I'll go you one better… He did it all just so no one would have to suffer the Second Death."

The conversation began taking an upward spiral as Tonika, rightfully puzzled, asked Etta Mae.

"What's the 'Second Death? …You can only die once. Now I do know that much. When you die, you're dead!"

Eve, finding the comedic exchange between the two a bit amusing leaned down addressing Tonika directly.

"O-oh, I see we have ourselves a baby Christian, huh? But don't you worry girlie. There're always eyes watching over you."

"What the—

Tonika jumps up recoiling from the specter's unsettling closeness.

"Oh girl." Etta Mae, calmly stroking her friend's arm interjected. "She just means God's eyes is always on you."

Then remembering her 'dream' added. "Oh yes! And those that make up that 'cloud of witnesses.' Including our visitor here."

And Evie, rest assured on my friend's convergence. I'm making doubly sure of that!"

"Very well then Miss Etta Mae. I was just checking I made the statement only because I cared."

"Y-You care?" Both women sputtered. "She cares!" The two laughed unbelievingly.

"What!" You think I'm so cold hearted that I don't care about mankind?"

The perplexed look on the women's faces led her to say.

"As all of you are aware, I made the wrong choice once, but I certainly paid for it!"

"Uh hmm, excuse me… but I think we've all paid for it." Tonika interjected.

"So sue me, as you all say!" Eve said. *"Even after my husband knew me, and I conceived again…"*

"Knew you? Tonika exclaimed. "You mean he didn't know who you were before? It won't but the two of you!"

"Tonika, if you would *please* …" Etta Mae said wearily. "It's just how they spoke in biblical times."

"Etta Mae, I'm sure glad you can read me, or shall I say; have read the Book."

She stole a glance at the clueless cohort.

"And just like the 'Creator' said, I brought forth my first born in pain."

She recalled the agony she'd suffered in childbirth and doubled over in imaginary pain.

"Oh! The pain of it all!"

Her actions evoked no sign of sympathy from Tonika, who soon lost interest in Eve's excuses for her long ago actions.

As far as she was concerned she couldn't in any form, or fashion, vindicate herself from the trauma of child bearing with no amount of explanation.

Donnie headed toward his bedroom, greatly anticipating a hot shower.

The voices he heard coming from the front of the house caused him to stop in his tracks. He turned and headed in their direction.

Tonika and his wife had been alone when he'd left the room earlier.

"Had someone come in while he and Dee were talking?"

With curiosity getting the better of him, he silently tipped down the hall and peered into the room.

What he saw caused him to fall back against the wall. Startled beyond belief, Donnie gasped for breath.

"I know you women curse me to this day!" Eve lamented. *"Even I could kick myself!"*

"Here let me do you the honors." Tonika said lifting her foot from the floor.

Eve avoided the extended foot just in time. Then with her gaze averted into the hallway she caught sight of the frightened man. The phantom woman stared deep into his eyes.

Etta Mae felt it was time to call a truce.

"Who, or better yet, what is that?" Donnie thought.

Beads of sweat ran down his temple. A barefoot, statuesque, Nubian figure clad in unidentifiable animal skin strutted back and forth, talking with Etta Mae and Tonika.

The far set eyes were enhanced with extended black lashes. Hair of coarse ropes fell mid-waist. A tilted nose protruded from a well chiseled face of wisdom and sat just above full, sensuous lips.

Ample breasts rose like two proud robins performing a mating ritual. All in all, the woman was something to behold.

"Wait a minute. Did I just hear them call her Eve?"

Nothing could have prepared him for this moment.

How could this be happening in his home?"

"Yep, there'd certainly been a breach like his wife had said this morning. *But,* the question is… *Why?*"

Donnie's assumption that the paranormal activity could play itself out when and wherever it desired had proven accurate.

"Oh, don't be so hard on yourself 'Evie girl,' it all worked out in the end.

It was already known by your heavenly Father what you were up against from the beginning. And that was… *Satan!*"

"I know what you mean, Etta Mae."

Eve reflected on how much she liked the way the woman thought. She even decided to address the time she had remaining specifically to Etta Mae.

For the life of her, Tonika could not understand exactly how she'd gotten caught up in this paranormal occurrence.

She had only come over to her 'BFF's to pour out her soul.

"Honey, no need to worry, God didn't intend for us to live in sin forever. And like you said, He'd already had a way to redeem Adam and me. Thank you LORD!

After the praise break she addressed the ladies once again.

"Ah ladies… Can I ask you a question?"

"That depends on what it is!" Tonika said, with eyes narrowed.

"Can you find it in your hearts to forgive me? After all, I am truly, truly, sorry."

This was all said of course with false humility. Eve's eyes were drawn to the bowl of fruit on the table. The ladies eyes followed her gaze as she reached for an apple.

"Can I have one of these?"

Tonika slapped at her hands.

"May I have?" Etta Mae corrected.

"Oh, for goodness sakes! May I have?"

After seizing the luscious fruit and taking a hefty bite, savoring its sweetness, Eve had this to say.

"Mmmmm ... Oh, by the way. Who said it was an apple I bit anyway?"

"What!" The two friends asked simultaneously.

Now you two ladies just wrap your heads around that one!"

Eve then turned to wink at Donnie before fading into oblivion, leaving the women to ponder the bombshell she'd just dropped.

The two friends sat dumbfounded while staring at the supernaturally vacated spot. Tonika, the first to gather her composure got up from the table.

It seemed to the formidable male in the hallway as if the specter had looked deep into the very core of his being.

Taking a deep intake of breath, Donnie shrinks back in fear. A wet puddle that had just happened to form in the exact spot where he'd been sitting made it necessary for a hasty retreat.

He reached the bedroom door, shutting it with a pronounced force, before finally giving way to mounted fear. He let out a loud yelp.

"Yo-owww!" Oh man, that was some scary shit out there!"

He couldn't seem to stop his knees from shaking.

"I can't believe it!" His mind traveled back to what had just happened.

"I saw it with my own eyes, but I still can't believe it. Oh, help me, Jesus!"

He thought of how his wife and Tonika appeared to have been lulled into some sort of a trance.

Surely by now, Dee would've sensed something. Why hadn't she come out of her room to investigate? But he would deal with the perplexity of it all, once he got cleaned up.

He stripped off his wet clothing and finally jumped into the refreshing shower.

"What was that noise?" The 'sleeping beauty queen' rose from the bed and went to the door.

"It sounded like someone yelling." She opened the door a crack and peered out.

The sound had come from the master bedroom. She was about to close the door again when she heard the voices of her sister and neighbor.

Dee stood there for a moment trying to decide if she should go out. Finally, she closed the door with her thoughts on how and what to tell her sister still fresh in her mind.

"Perhaps, I need to talk with someone else first, like a pastor maybe, before making any decisions."

The chat with her brother-in-law had helped a little. He hadn't been too judgmental.

True, he was shocked to hear what little she'd told him, but alas, it's the way of the world.

She approached the bed once again. The decision of what she would do had been made.

"I'll just finish my nap; later I'll take a walk around the neighborhood to clear my head.

Then maybe I'll look for a church whose doors may just happen to be open."

"Yes, that's what I'll do. After all, this thing is too big for me. Maybe it will take a man of the cloth to make everything plain."

With her mind in a well-deserved state of euphoria, Dee drifted off to sleep once again.

CHAPTER
Eleven

....

"I can't believe what just happened!" Tonika lashed out. "That heifer just pops out just like she popped in. "Can you find it in your heart to forgive me?" What nerve!"

Etta Mae looked on with disinterest, not caring to add to the charade.

"And did you see how flippant she was acting? And just what was that last comment about?

Everyone knows it was an apple she took from that tree. It was, wasn't it Etta Mae?"

The befuddled neighbor slightly shoved her seemingly traumatized cohort to bring her out of a stupor.

"What do you think the fruit was?" Tonika paced back and forth.

"Huh, what?"

"The fruit, Etta Mae, what was it?"

"The fruit... the fruit, let's see." Etta Mae pondered the matter. "Hmmm... I don't know, maybe it was a fig. The Bible does say they covered themselves with a fig leaf."

"A fig, you think?"

"All I know is, there's a lot of talk about fig trees in the Bible, but I haven't heard of, not to my knowledge anything about any apple trees."

"Fig, apple, turnip!" Tonika razzed. "What's the point?"

"Of course I could be wrong. So don't quote me on it. I just might have to research that one."

"And old Evie-Eve should be sorry, as much pain I went through giving birth to that nine-pound big-headed boy of mine!"

"Tonika… get a grip; get a hold of yourself!"

"Etta Mae, I'm serious! And you ought to be glad you stopped me from getting my hands on her old butt… I would have rung her flipping neck!"

Etta Mae looked on her friend with amusement.

"Your boy did have a big old head!"

They each found that statement hilarious, and filled the room with hysterics.

After which, Etta Mae voiced a concern that had just entered her mind.

"Sa-ay girl, I wonder if any more unwanted guests will pop in today." Tonika said, eerily surveying the room.

"I certainly hope not, I don't think I could stand it. And besides, don't be laughing at my sweet pea… That's my little munchkin; big head and all."

"You know it does hurt pushing those little boogers into the world. But once you look into those little faces; you forget all about the pain you went through. Now am I right?"

Etta Mae smiled broadly as she thought of the birth of her daughter Janet. Yes, she could truly identify with the sentiments of her friend.

Each time they spoke with their daughter, 'Granddaddy Wann'a Be' always anticipated hearing "Surprise, we're pregnant!"

Tonika's voice bought Etta Mae back to focus.

"You're right. If only they could stay that little and innocent!" "That's exactly right. If only—

An annoying fly constantly buzzed Etta Mae's head. She absentmindedly swatted at it.

"And they look like little rats when you first see them. Don't they?"

Tonika couldn't help but take notetook note of Etta Mae's efforts with the annoying pest.

"Girl what is with you and that fly?"

"With me-e, what's up with it?" Etta Mae said getting up to search for her fly swatter.

"Where is that darn fly swatter when you need it?"

"It's probably where you last swatted 'the old Broomstick'!"

"Stop it girl. You're too much today. Etta laughingly said before adding. "Hey, you know what my friend?"

"What!"

"I didn't feel right having that 'close encounter of the third kind' pop up like that! I should call my husband maybe he's out of the shower by now."

"Now honey I'm with 'ya there. At first, I was shaking in my boots!"

A tingling sensation ran down Tonika's spine. She shuddered in her seat.

"Yes, but you soon got over it;then you became a tyrant."

"I did, didn't I! Wonder where all my courage came from?"

"I don't know, but what do you think would happen if we started talking about you know who?

"Who?"

"Beelzebub, the 'Lord of the flies!'"

"For the sake of all that is holy, honey, please don't bring him up!"

Wednesday's Bible study came to mind. A discussion of Mark 3:22, where the Pharisees accused Jesus of driving out demons by the power of Beelzebub the prince of demons.

It had felt creepy discussing it then, and it felt even creepier now that the morning's weird encounter had occurred. And yes, there was still that annoying fly.

"If you don't!" Tonika swatted at the same fly. "Now the darn thing is buzzing my head!"

The annoying visitor would light long enough to send each woman ducking and dodging. Then the flying nuisance would lift off. This went on for quite some time.

The frustrated 'keeper of her castle' wadded a newspaper to the stand in for the elusive fly swatter.

"Here! Let me have a go at him."

Whack!

The fly however, sensed his impending doom and had reacted just in time by flying a short distance out of harm's way.

"Ouch!"

The weapon of choice had missed its target, but had landed solidly on Tonika's head.

"Darn! I missed it!"

"Yes, you did, but you gave me a concussion in the process. *Dang! Thanks! Friend."*

The unfortunate receiver of the wayward blow said while gingerly rubbing the pulsating area.

"I'm sorry, here; let Mama kiss it and make it all better."

"No, thanks, that won't be necessary."

Tonika putting out a hand blocks the unwelcomed gesture.

"Well, I tried…"

"Yes, you did try. But wasn't that creepy how that thing kept going from you, then to me?"

The creepy invader eventually, lifted off its safety perch, and flew out of the room.

"Something wasn't quite right about it, I know that." Etta Mae said. "I didn't want to spook you, so I didn't say anything."

"Well, honey, you can consider me spooked!" That was scary! And it may've been my imagination, but I could've sworn that thing looked me dead in my eye!"

"I know, right! I think it's time to bring out the smoking gun!"

Etta Mae said rising from the table like a woman on a mission.

"And that would be?"

"Why, the B-I-B-L-E! And not only that, but I'm going to hit that fly with a double whammy!"

"Oh, my! That thing's going to rue the day he messed with Etta Mae Collins Smith!"

"Now you're right about that!"

The 'spiritual crusader' anointed every surface with extra virgin olive oil and prayed as she went.

"There! That should really hit the pest where it hurts."

"He had it coming, messing with the 'demon buster' in her own home!" Tonika excitedly added.

"You know what, after all this; I think I need to get some fresh air. What about you?"

"Yes Lord! What do you have in mind?"

"I don't know about you, but nothing would clear my head better than a good old shopping spree!

What do you say we do some damage in Kolkrofts today?"

"Girl, you're on; I'll be right back!"

Tonika managed to jump up despite having wobbly legs and headed for the door.

Etta Mae looked toward the bedroom.

"I won't bother my honey; hopefully, he has taken his shower by now and is probably fast asleep."

She decided to scribble a note to inform him of her whereabouts. Etta Mae knew her sister would be long asleep, after complaining of being disturbed this morning.

"Honey, I'm gone!"

After retrieving her purse from the sofa table in the living room, Etta Mae quietly left the house, sliding easily into the sleek gray 2000 Audi S4.

Tonika ran back from across the street; now satisfied her son had left for his practice. A little winded, she settled into the passenger seat.

The supple luxury charcoal gray leather seats readily molded to the women's frames.

The captain at the helm manipulated the sound system from the steering column, locating her favorite station.

Merging into the flowing traffic was little problem for the purring 2.8 litre engine. The Twilight Mall in nearby Ragnarok, New Jersey was the anticipated destination.

It was a fifteen-minute car ride from their neighborhood.

Surprisingly, few words were exchanged between the car's occupants.

They each were deep in thought, neither wanted to break the emotionally charged silence.

Along with the supernatural visit by Eve this morning, Dee's situation was a point of stress for Etta Mae.

Meanwhile, her friend struggled with the decision of whether to share her marriage turmoil.

When she'd first gone over she had been about ready to cry on her compassionate neighbor's shoulder, but that had all changed.

Tonika nervously glanced over at her dear friend, desperately wanting to release the tightness in her chest. But the pink element that once moved so freely, now remained cleaved to the roof of her mouth.

The luxury sedan sliced effortlessly through the air like a bullet destined for its target.

After a seemingly endless ride, they finally pulled into the east parking lot of the Twilight Mall.

The ladies exited and aimlessly surveyed the parking lot dotted with late model sedans. Even a Hummer, or two were situated here and there.

"Boy… You sure couldn't tell it by this parking lot full of new cars that we're in a recession."

"Good ole c.c. doesn't realize we're in a recession."

"Now what pray tell does a gospel singer have to do with all these cars. Is she in concert?"

"No girl!" Etta Mae said. "I meant credit cards!"

"Oh, okay, I'm with you now."

"Look at it this way; as long as your credit's good you can have the world!"

The two women shared a much-needed laugh.

"I need to go into Peony's. Ashad is growing out of clothes faster than a weed in a compost heap!"

Tonika adjusting the strap of her shoulder bag looked up in time to see a familiar female figure hurrying their way.

CHAPTER

"*Y*a' ought 'a be starting somethin—ought 'a be starting some-thin—
Un, un, un, un, um. Mm, mm, mm, mm, mm."

Tangoing his way to the refrigerator the jubilant gardner loudly sang.

Now alone in the house, Donnie readied himself for a relaxing, most enjoyable, Saturday afternoon.

The adjacent neighbor's cat had been seen prowling the yard. The homeowner kept a watchful eye on his prized pond where colorful Japanese koi swam sedately, oblivious to any pending doom.

Etta Mae had long since left for the mall. He hadn't even gotten a chance to discuss the excitement of the morning with either her, or his sister-in-law.

She had left before he could come out of the room, but had left a note to say that she and Tonika had gone shopping.

Donnie hadn't wanted to stress his sister-in-law out any more than she already was. After she had awakened and showered, he'd simply put a key in her hand and told her to have a pleasant walk. He had warned her to be careful and alert.

Admittedly, he was all too eager to settle into his familiar routine of watching a favorite television show, 'Where Angels Tread.' But still, his mind couldn't seem to shake the morning's eerie occurrence.

"What was the world coming to?" He wondered.

"Paranormal activity everywhere; spirits popping up at every whim."

Donnie mentally recalled the image of a book he'd casually browsed through, while waiting for his wife to finalize a purchase at Binders Christian Bookstore.

On the books cover was a smiling woman with her hands raised to Heaven. The book's title, *"Heaven… A Time Travel Away,"* had intrigued him enough to warrant his reading a few paragraphs.

Apparently, this woman had been visited by Jesus who had taken her spirit on an out of this world journey. On her journey, she'd glimpsed a moment of Hell.

The woman stated she hadn't been afraid because the Lord was with her. But the woman was saddened to see so many people she'd known in such ahorrible place.

Jesus had then escorted her to Heaven. She had stated that the immense beauty of the place was too indescribable to mention.

"It has to be all the accelerated interests in the paranormal that these weird things are happening. We just keep messing with those 'hants.' The patient spouse concluded. "They know they ought-a quit!"

He shuddered and looked around the spacious kitchen.

"Who ya' goin 'a call? Ghost Busters! *Ha, ha, ha.*"

Donnie would have to hurry if he wanted to watch the special episode he really wanted to see, according to the clock on the stove.

Donnie waved away a buzzing fly that circled his head. He peered into the chrome finished double door refrigerator.

He visually checked off the necessary ingredients needed to make up a self-proclaimed double 'D' sandwich, known as the 'Donnie Detonator.' The proud sous-chef of his own kitchen personally claimed full rights to the overstuffed concoction.

"Let's see here; sourdough bread, check—Cotto salami, check—honey glazed ham, check—shredded lettuce, tomatoes—Check and…check!"

"Ooh, boy, my little secret ingredient, you are a tad too ripe."

Donnie lifted the lid, but closed it just as quickly.

"Alright then, dill pickles! Yumm! Banana peppers, Cheddar and Swiss cheese, and…Ah yes, my pretty little Pro-vo-lone."

Then placing all the trappings of his mouth-watering delight on the counter, Donnie returned to the refrigerator for condiments.

"Now where is my special salad dressing?"

Donnie reached for his other secret ingredient hidden behind a jar of black olives.

"Come on baby its eating time!"

He moved ketchup, olive bottles, and left over spaghetti in a plastic container, only to find the jar empty.

"What? I can't believe it. It's empty! *Et-ta!*" He shouted in the air. "I sure hope you're grocery shopping!"

He picked up a jar of mustard. "I guess this mustard will have to do. But darn, it just won't be the same."

Highly disappointed, Donnie now eyed the mouth watering chicken salad his wife had made for tomorrow's church auxiliary luncheon.

He'd watched her mix the sour cream, salad dressing, celery, onions, boiled eggs, pickle relish and other ingredients in with the cooled diced chicken. The salad was one of his wife's most coveted dishes at the church.

"Humph, unless I have a death wish I'd better not touch you. I certainly don't want to hear my wife's mouth."

He finally constructed the deli delight with heightened anticipation. A tall glass of sweetened iced tea was next on the menu.

After making his way across the room, Donnie picked up the television remote. He was poised to sit in his favorite chair when the doorbell rang.

"Oh, *man!*" He said irritated at being interrupted. "Now who could that be?"

The first thing he thought was perhaps his sister-in-law had forgotten her key, but then he remembered personally placing it directly in her palm.

"I don't know who it could be then, but I sure don't feel like being bothered!"

The doorbell rang again. Donnie turned down the volume. He looked first toward the door then back to the television and remained perfectly still. He was resigned to the fact that it probably wasn't for him anyway.

"It's probably for my wife. Everyone I know is still on the golf course. Maybe, if I don't answer whoever it is will go away."

99

Persistent knocking followed his assumption. An immense sigh escaped his lips. He reluctantly took his tray back to the kitchen.

"Don't go anywhere, 'cause I will be back for you later."

Donnie went to the front door and shouted.

"Who is it? Etta Mae's not home!"

"It's Damien!"

The voice on the other side of the solid oak four-paneled door responded.

"Damien Whitman. Is this the Smith's home?"

Damien' was all Donnie heard. "Oh *Lord!* It's the devil himself! Oh no! Here we go!"

He had just watched an episode of the 1976 movie, 'The Omen, on Monday night. An American ambassador had learned to his horror, that his son was the literal 'Antichrist.'

"Oh, Lord! Lord!"

Donnie grabbed at his chest as his heart raced a mile a minute.

"O, Lord! The old soul-snatcher has come for me! I'm going Etta Mae! Bye honey."

The knocking and doorbell ringing still persisted. The vigilant fly watched from its perch on the back of the leather seat where the cantankerous host had been about to sit.

"First, it was that animal skinned wearing incarnated ghost, and now him!"

"What am I going to do now?" Donnie lamented. Then he thought.

"*Wait!* I can't go yet, at least not with him!"

This was a frightening situation. The panic-stricken man then began to pace in front of the closed door. He didn't deal too easily with fear.

"Listen, 'Old Slew Foot', if you're looking for my wife, she's not here!"

"*Slew Foot?*" The perplexed visitor shouted.

Damien was at a loss in deciphering what exactly could be happening on the other side of the door.

"Listen man… I'm not looking for Etta Mae, but I am looking for—

"Then, uh, surely you're not looking for me! I don't have any dealings with you. I went to church last Sunday, and I'm definitely going tomorrow!"

"Man! What are you rambling on about?"

Damien couldn't believe what He was hearing. Placing both hands on either side of the Doorpost and leaning in with his face only inches away yelled through the door.

"I'm not looking for Etta Mae, or you for that matter...*but,* I am looking for my wife!"

"Your wife?" Donnie asked unbelievingly. "You have a wife?"

"Are you going to let me in and stop all this *bull,* or what?"

"*No!* You can't come in here. I plead the blood of Jesus! You can't have my soul. *Satan!* Get thee behind me; or better still get under my feet!"

"Or, at least get under my feet."

The weak spot on the wood floor creaked as the nervous man paced. The creaking only added to the freaky dilemma he found himself in.

"He's come for me...Oh Lord, where did I go wrong? I pray, I tithe, I ...

Becoming even more frantic he began calling for his wife.

"*Etta Mae*! Where are you? I need you now!" "You need who now?"

The heated visitor looked threateningly toward the door and asked another question.

"And why are you calling me Satan? You don't know me." "Well, I-I just naturally assumed..."

"Brotha,' believe me... I just come for my wife! And you know what they say about assuming."

Taking a deep breath, lowering his voice Damien contemplated on what to do next.

The irritated visitor chose to knock even more persistently.

On the inside of the door, a recollection of sorts suddenly took place.

"Oh! That's right, his wife ...Dee! Oh man!"

Donnie gave his forehead an open handed smack.

"How stupid of me, this must be Dee's current husband."

As Donnie pondered the matter, he asked himself.

"But was his name... Damien? I can't remember what she said it was."

The confused homeowner wiped the sweat from his brow and began composing himself.

Apparently, the morning's encounter had affected him more than he cared to think.

"Whew! Thank God!"

A feeling of relief flooded over the grateful man as he said to himself.

"You just cannot keep up with that woman's men folk!"

"Yo!"

The front door finally swung open with a sheepish grin plastered on the embarrassed greeter's face.

"C-can I help you?"

At that exact time, the same mysterious fly chose to conveniently exit the premises.

The loud buzzing sound of its beating wings caused both men to duck and dodge.

Damien Whitman, a tall trimmed specimen of a man with lines of neat and pleasing symmetry stood at the door. He was dressed in a casual crisp beige linen shirt opened at the collar.

The long lean legs were housed in the finest linen slacks that topped the tan 'Testoni Norvese' leather loafers.

The gold Rolex watch caught the light of the afternoon sun, sending a blinding flash into the room.

The dapper gentleman pushed past the peculiar host. His eyes ran to and fro as he frantically called for his humiliated spouse.

"Delilah, Delilah!"

Donnie tried to halt the intruder by grabbing hold of his arm, but was no match for the mass of muscles.

"Hold up, dude; slow your roll!"

"Man back up off me!" The highly miffed intruder barked.

"Where is my wife?"

Jerking free and staring menacingly at the equally perturbed homeowner the irate intruder once again shouted.

"I said, where is my wife? I know she's here!"

"Whoa there Bro! You don't know jack!"

Donnie was prepared to block what blow he thought might come his way.

"Damn it! You can't just waltz up in here like a linebacker out of hell! Besides, your wife ain't here!"

"This is the home of Etta Mae Smith isn't it?"

"Yes, it is."

"Hmmm... I don't know, maybe Delilah just hasn't arrived here yet... but I know she's bound to come sometime or other."

A tad satisfied, but mostly disappointed the somewhat relieved visitor turned to leave.

Donnie saw the look of disappointment on the distraught man's face, decided to throw him an ounce of hope.

"She's here, but she's not here."

"What exactly are you saying, dude?"

Donnie then went on to explain why he had delayed opening the door.

"To tell you the truth, you had me scared for a moment, w-when you said you were Damien."

He had to chuckle at the thought himself.

"I thought you were s-someone else. You know what I mean?"

"Oo-oh! Now I get it."

At first Damien was perplexed, but it soon registered what the now settled man was actually saying. In any case he was somewhat relieved he'd finally found his runaway spouse's whereabouts.

"Y-you mean you were expecting my boy Lucifer? Man, that's dope!" Damien laughed.*"Ha, ha, ha."*

"Hey, you never know!" Believe me when I tell you....after what I've seen today; anything can happen up in here!"

"I sure don't know what's been happening, but... people have joked about me being the 'devil' for some time. So you're not the first; believe me when I tell you."

"How did you feel about having that name?"

"Or...they'd ask if my Mom was into voodoo, or some stupid shit like that!"

"Well, you do have to admit, it's not a name I would be proud of."

"I live with it, that's what I do."

"I know you saw that 70's movie didn't you? Wait a minute, on second thought, exactly how old are you?"

"Dude… what movie? And what does my age have to do with some damn movie?" The frustrated man walked away.

"I just thought I'd ask."

"If you must know, I'm thirty-nine.

"Well, okay then; I just thought you may have been too young to know what I was talking about.

"Humph, I highly doubt it."

"The movie I'm speaking of is the one where this young boy was possess—never mind. Unless you watched it Monday night."

"No, I didn't watch anything on Monday night."

"Well, okay then." Donnie's mind drifted back to the visitor's name. "No I wouldn't particularly be too proud to be called Damien."

"Look, could we just get off my name. I've lived with it this long, and I'll continue to live with it so…."

"Now, you do know what your name means don't you?"

Donnie could not miss an opportunity to show his expert opinion in obsolete topics

"Nope, I hadn't given it any thought whatsoever. But, I'm sure Mr. 'Walking Encyclo'is about to tell me!"

"W-ell… the opinionator said, drawing out the word. "Damien is a boy's name. But get this. It can also be used as a gi-rrl's name also."

Donnie hid a snicker behind his hand.

"And your point is?" Damien asked with a raised brow.

"Oh; nothing just that it comes from the Greek and it means "to tame, to subdue.

Now you're going to love this one. The Greek root of Damien can also mean 'spirit' or something close to it."

"Would you please cut it out? Man… Damn!" "Okay, homie….Sorry."

Donnie hadn't wanted to irritate the unexpected visitor any further, but he felt compelled to repeat the question that still lingered in the air.

"Now, let me get this straight; my wife's sister, Dee is your wife."

"Dee? Delilah Whitman you mean?"

"What do you want with…Dee?"

Donnie stepped around the house guest and settled on the couch.

"Would you quit stalling?"

Damien took a seat adjacent to his host.

"I-I'm not going to hurt her if that's what you're asking. I just don't know where else she could've gone. She just left so fast!"

"I wonder why?" Donnie said under his breath.

"What was that?" Damien harshly inquired. He'd attempted to lift himself up but remained seated.

"Why—what has she told you?"

"Nothing, Brotha Man; not a thing, so just take it easy!"

Allowing his arm to rest on the chair's arm, Donnie looked with disdain at the troubled soul.

Donnie had hoped his words would somehow calm the demons raging war in the man's soul.

"Your wife was here."

"Would you just spell it out and quit the bull crap!"

"I mean she arrived here late yesterday. But don't ask me where she is now." Donnie threw up both his hands.

"You're saying you don't know where she is, but… Come on, I hear a 'but' in your voice."

"All I know is she left a short time after my wife. She got up from her nap, and said she wanted to clear her head. So, off she went."

"Once again, she just up and left."

This news irritated the deserted husband even further. He jumped to his feet, and begun to pace the floor.

"That seems to be her thing lately. Just up and left! Didn't even tell me she was gone!"

"Well it wasn't exactly my day to keep up with your woman."

The nervous ranting caused a little uneasiness in Donnie.

"Heck, I can't even keep up with my own wife let alone yours."

Then he thought of something that had been said.

"Wait a minute; you said you flew in this morning…Then what took you so long to get here?"

The early flight had allowed Damien time to sit and think. He had been torn between boarding a return flight allowing matters to ride as they were, or find his wife and throw himself on her mercy.

He had finally decided on booking a hotel room.

"Yes, I came home from work to discover she'd packed her bags and had taken off. I figured she'd come here; she always talked about her big sister Etta Mae."

"How'd you know my address and how to find this house?"

"I'd looked in my wife's Rolodex, then I rented a car with a GPS and it brought me right to your door." "Well, you just may be in luck."

Donnie felt a tinge of empathy for the distressed man's plight. He hoped his next words would offer a ray of hope.

"Look, I don't think she's gone too far. She didn't leave with a suitcase or anything."

"Good!" Then that means she's coming back."

Donnie chuckled before he added.

"I take it, you find the situation amusing." Damien looked at the smirking man with a look to kill. "Well there's nothing funny about it!"

"I'm just saying, you know women and their shoes; and the ones your wife had on won't let her get too far, believe me."

Damien talked more to himself than to his host.

"I've got to explain… and she'll accept my explanation. Yes, she just has to!"

"Oh, she does, aye? Let me ask you something, 'Bubba'… Do you think you can?"

Donnie was skeptical. "I don't think there's that much explaining in the world!"

"Oh? Why'd you say that?"

"Think about it. Would you if the shoe were on the other foot?"

Damien was at a loss for words. It just could be that he was expecting too much from his wife after what he'd put her through. But, yet, he could still hope.

"Listen! I don't know what to tell you. All I know is I can't even explain what's been going on in my house, let alone your situation! Ghosts popping out of the woodwork and—

"What! What ghost?"

The casual remark had caught the wayfaring visitor off guard.

Donnie was pleased. He had meant for his statement to be a distraction. A well timed ploy had often served as a great coping method for many of his golfing buddies' marital dilemmas.

"Your house haunted or something, dude?"

Damien looked around the room as if seeing it for the first time.

"What house isn't haunted?" Donnie said. "Unless you built it from the ground up, you never know who died in it."

"Believe me, I for damn sure would know." Damien said.

"There is a law that says a seller has to disclose it if a death had occurred in a home before it's purchased." "Oh, is that right?"

"But still, even then you couldn't be sure ... the home could have been built over an old cemetery, you never know."

"As much as I hate to say it, you could be right."

The movie 'Poltergeist' Damien had seen as a young boy came to mind.

"No wonder you thought I was the devil!" He jumped toward Donnie and shouted. "Boooo!"

"*Ohh!* Fool, don't do that to me!"

"Sorry, but I couldn't resist. And the look on your face was priceless! *Ha, ha, ha!*"

"Well I'm still not convinced you're not!" Donnie emphatically stated.

"Well, I'm not! And as far as that goes, you're the one who's seeing ghosts!"

"Okay, okay, you got me there, 'Brotha' Man." Donnie said, relenting. "I don't know what to make of it."

"Believe me when I have to tell you, had it been me, I would definitely know!"

"Well... all I know is that I went to take a shower, when I heard a voice other than Etta Mae's and Tonika's.

So, when I came down the hall to investigate, the two women were having 'hissy' fits."

"Tonika, now who is she? And where was Delilah?"

"Tonika is my wife's best friend, our neighbor from across the street, or I should say, the pest from across the street."

"Look man, this is some scary you know what, going on up in here. And you did look as if you'd seen a ghost when I came in."

"I'm not ashamed to admit it. I've really been frightened today."

"And what was up with your friend;the fly?"

"The heck if I know! At least he flew out. *Dang it...* I sure hope the bastard didn't land his butt on my sandwich!"

"You can bet on it, that's what flies do you know."

"Oh crap! Along with you, he had to pop up! I betch'a he ruined my dang sandwich!"

"Sorry; my bad."

"Course now, in these days and times everything's popping up... and coming out. Gays and ghosts! Flies, and— gays." Donnie said, smirking.

"Man!" Damien huffed. He'd chosen to ignore the gaunt chap's latest remark.

"I don't know if I want to be here with you. So just give me my wife and I'm out 'a here!"

"Shucks, it's getting to the point I'm almost afraid to be in my own home; let alone you being afraid."

They eyed the room skeptically. Donnie's face is overcome with feigned fear.

"Etta-a Mae... Come home!"

"*Ha, ha, ha*! What's a big boy like you doing being afraid of a little ole ghost?

Damien found the man's fearful demeanor hilarious.

"Boo!" He shouted once again.

"Yo, Bro,'what's up with that fear you have going there?"

He covered his mouth to hide a grin.

"Say... I wouldn't be laughing if I were you, because you're surely in for a rude awakening. And from what I hear, you sure could use a little awakening."

Donnie walked into the dining area. He had missed lunch and wanted to check on his sandwich that was sure to be stale.

"Rude awakening?"

Damien asked as he followed closely on the retreating man's heels. Donnie abruptly stopped and the two collided.

"Damn, are you smoking weed or something?" Damien asked as he backed off. "What does my being awaken have to do with anything?"

"Oh, it's nothing dude."

Donnie knew they could go on for hours berating each other. Turning to face his house guest Donnie extended his right hand for a handshake.

"Tell you what partner, enough with all this crazy talk. Let's just start all over... Okay?"

"You're on!" Damien shook the extended hand of truce.

CHAPTER
Thirteen

....

"A compost heap, Tonika really!" Etta Mae said as her eyes followed her friend's gaze. They absentmindedly waved to the approaching figure.

"Girl you know you do have a way with words.

"Well thank you, I'd like to think so."

"Ashad really is growing like a string bean though. When last I saw him and Josh on Tuesday, the boy was tall and gangly."

Knowing the close relationship Josh had shared with Ashad was now ended caused a pained look on Tonika's face. She stifled the sob that was rising up from the recesses of her soul.

Stephanie Willis eagerly greeted them with outstretched arms before Etta Mae could comment.

Stephanie had a flamboyant personality and talked in run-on sentences. The two ladies had realized early on just how pointless it was in trying to get a word in edgewise.

"Hey, Sistah Girls! How have you two been, and what have you been up to?"

The woman's medium built slender frame was softly draped in a crème colored ruffled tank dress that rose mid-thigh. Small ear lobes were burdened with heavy 'Silverstone' owl earrings that hung just below the well defined jaw line.

Shuffling her weight from side to side, Stephanie seemingly towered six inches taller than her usual 5'5" stature. This was thanks mostly to the six inch 'pretty, purple, peep-toe' Prata high heel shoes.

"Are you guys boycotting the gas pumps too; or Etta Mae, did you drive that fine gray Audi?"

She peered behind the ladies and spotted the alluded vehicle.

"Yes, I—

"Oh, I see, never mind….Tonika, how you like riding in that fine ride… how does it ride?"

"It's rides smooth—

"Umph, Can I say I left my car in the garage? I certainly won't about to drive that old gas-aholic of mine; not with the bus driving right past my apartment too!"

The neighbors exchanged knowing glances.

"It just does not make any sense with gas prices being the way they are."

Etta Mae and Tonika shifted their feet from right to left.

"Gas is $5.00 a gallon! Can you believe it? There just ought to be a law! People, I swear!"

Stephanie's over exuberant excessive chatter continued on. Tonika hurriedly interrupted, hoping to slow the flow.

"Stephanie, girl, I love those shoes. And you got them from 'FSP' didn't you?"

"Girl, now, how'd you guess?" Stephanie shrieked. "Yes, they're from the 'FSPs', the Fabulous Shoe Palace!"

By turning her head, Etta Mae hid a smirk as she covered her mouth with her hand.

"You guys going to the shoe sale? I'm telling you, honey, I hit those sales like a ball hitting a bat!"

Then thinking better of what she'd just said.

"Uh, I meant, a bat hitting a ball… well, you know what I mean."

"Yeah girl, we know exactly what you mean. You were on that sale like spots on a cheetah!"

Etta Mae gave Tonika a playful nudge and they both laughed.

"I know that's right." Tonika added.

"Boy, it sure is warm out here!"

Stephanie frantically fanned her face with her hands.

"Yes it is, and we should be getting out of this heat."

Etta Mae declared, taking a step forward to do just that.

Just as they were about to make their way to the mall's entrance, a Black LS 460 Lexus, honked. The driver waved to the three companions. The car was driven by a Mrs. Porter, a well to do philanthropist from the east-side.

Stephanie returned the wave, but she couldn't help but share a bit of gossip with the girls. She watched the luxury sedan weave its way thru the parking lot and then began.

"O, Lord, now will you look at that! Humph, Mizz Porter. Now ain't she something, driving around like Mizz Goldfinger. If it was me, I would go into that big house and not come out!"

"You would say that Miss Coveting Cora. From where I'm standing, it did look to me she was friendly enough towards you." Etta Mae stated. "I just happen to think the woman is rather nice."

"Uh, huh, if you say so." Stephanie interjected.

"Well, it looked that way to *me*." Etta Mae added. "Plus, she didn't have to wave at your old butt, you know!"

"Yeah, she's nice in her own way." Tonika added. "You just have to get to know her is all. Besides, she can't help it if she's been super blessed. Humph, we should all be so lucky."

"Girl, sounds like you've had the distinct pleasure of meeting her."

"Yep, I have! And it just so happens that she's my soror, so back up off my sistah!"

"I never knew that!" Etta Mae bellowed, looking at her friend in a state of wonder. "Girl, you never cease to amaze me."

"Remind me to talk to you about it later, okay?"

"Yes, we certainly must talk."

"Ah-umf!" Stephanie cleared her throat to bring the focus back to Mrs. Porter.

"Well, I'm glad for your upcoming talking appointment, but I do hope you know, looks *can* be deceiving."

She leaned in and whispered.

"You haven't heard the latest on your girl now have you?"

"No, I hadn't heard anything. Have you Tonika?"

"No, not lately…So what's 'ole Miss 'P' supposedly done now?"

"Well…"

Now that she had their interest, the rumormonger proceeded to share the latest gossip she'd acquired.

"My Bobbie told me that she tried to corner her landscaper into going to bed with her."

"*Shut up!* Girl, you lying! She did what?!" Tonika shouted, shocked at the news.

"Now why would she do that?" Etta Mae inquired, giving Stephanie a disapproving look.

"Why would a high society dame like her do something so callous?"

"Now I do not believe that." Tonika said. "Stephanie is just trying to start something. Besides, that woman has a husband.

And not only a husband, but a pretty damn rich one at that! Now run and tell that!" She snapped her fingers in Stephanie's face.

Stephanie rolled her eyes, then staunchly folded her arms and allowed all her weight to rest on one foot defiantly said to her skeptics.

"So what; like that's going to stop anybody! Since when has being married ever stopped the 'red rooster' from tromping on the neighbor's spotted hens?" Then she added."Aye, To-ni-ka?"

"W-Wha-at?" Taken aback, Tonika gasped.

Satisfied by the shocked reaction she'd invoked, Stephanie continued with her supposedly accountable information.

"Ummph, they said the old girl called Josiah; that's his name you know in her mansion. She'd pretended her petunias were wilting.

They say she snuck up behind my man Joe, and grabbed him. But, all she got was coat, because they say boyfriend shot out of there so fast!

I don't blame him though, 'cause I know he does not; I repeat does-not-want-to-tackle the Porter dude."

Stephanie's guttural laughter rang through the parking lot.

Etta Mae couldn't help but find the humor in the storytelling, but the humor was lost on her befuddled colleague. The insinuated remark made earlier still had her flustered.

"Exactly what did Stephanie mean by saying that?" Tonika pondered. "Does she know something I should know?"

She searched the talebearer's eyes inquiringly, only to receive a mere wink, followed with a silently mouthed; "We'll talk... Call me."

"Here, let me give you my cell number."

Tonika fished around in her purse and came up with a pen, which she stuck in her mouth while hunting for a piece of paper.

Etta Mae looked questionably from one woman to the other, but neither offered any explanation.

Stephanie furnished Tonika with a business card from her purse and picked up where she'd left off with Mrs. Porter.

"Thank you."

"Uh, huh... They say that man's got connections, and I'm not just talking *business* connections either. If you know what I mean. Rat-a-tat-tat-tat!" The animated storyteller made to emphasize.

"Well... Mr. Porter is gone a lot." Tonika added defensively. He's always traveling, and I do hope they are business trips."

In a barely audible breath, she added. "I guess the poor girl does get lonesome."

The conversation was beginning to hit too close to home, so with a feigned cheerfulness, Tonika then exclaimed.

"Plus, you know what they say, "when the cat's away, the mouse will... "*Pla-ay... He-ey!*"

They all chimed in laughing hard. This called for high five between the three acquaintances. Etta Mae had to jump to reach their highly extended hands.

"Now, you two know you're wrong. How're you going to make me jump like that? But Stephanie, girl your story reminds me of something similar."

"It does...like what?"

"It reminds me of—

"Shucks, that's no excuse because the man traveled so much. He has to keep a roof over that coiffured head. Besides you know my girl's hair is never out of place."

"Minds you of what, Etta Mae?" Tonika didn't wait for her friend's response but addressed her next statement to Stephanie instead.

"Not only a roof honey, but you saw what she was driving, and she certainly wasn't trying to save any gas!"

She and Stephanie touched fists and laughed.

"Yes, and did you two notice what her custom tags read?"

Etta Mae felt a bit miffed witnessing the familiarity shared between the two.

"It said, 'DON'T H-8-T'… Don't hate! So don't hate you two! And besides! My 'Boo' did just fine by me with my, Ow! Ow! Au-di!"

Tonika sensed Etta Mae's annoyance.

"Etta Mae, girl, you're standing in a parking lot just like us… So why're you going there?"

"You're right, I am standing in the parking lot, but I'm *trying* to go into the mall! And! I ain't hating… Or better yet, I'm not coveting a Lexus either."

"And neither are we!" Tonika said, just as pointedly. "But we were merely making an observation!"

"Ah, heck, that's why snooty people drive those old damn elite machines anyways." Stephanie added. "Just so they can front and so other people can gawk."

"Now, you're right about that!" Tonika agreed.

"And you know for yourself those people are saying, "Look at what I've got, don't you wish it was yours?"

"That may be true, but all I'm saying is material things and luxuries of this world are only temporary." Etta Mae said to drive her point home.

"But, only what you do for Christ will last! Tonika, now you do know where I'm going with this don't 'cha?"

"Uh-Oh, here we go!" Tonika jokingly said to Stephanie.

"Let me guess… Could it be the Bible?"

She threw up her hands in surrender.

"I swear! Etta Mae and her living WORD! Stephanie, this woman is the only one I know that can bring that book to life! And I mean literally bring it to life."

This conversation was lost on the Bible illiterate 'club hopper.' Stephanie's knowledge of the 'good book' could be measured with a six inch ruler.

"Where are you going with this, Etta Mae?" Stephanie inquired. "You keep mentioning—

Tonika playfully grabbed Stephanie by the arm.

"Girl! I'm warning you!"

"What?"

The phenomenon virgin thought the women were merely joking, and had begun to laugh.

"That's right they do call it *the Living Word,* don't they?"

The complex conversation had become a bit too disturbing to the baffled woman, so Tonika felt the need to recount their morning's escapade.

"We're not joking girlfriend. Just this morning we had a ghostly visitation. We were visited by the first lady herself."

"Stop lying girl!" The paranormal skeptic bowled over with laughter once again. "Michelle Obama ain't been to your house!" Y'all are some fools!"

"No dunce! I'm talking about the very *first* woman; Eve. Whenever my friend here begins to talk Bible… well you just wait."

"Wait for what…and did you say Eve… like Adam's Eve? Like the hussy who bit that apple?"

"Uh-huh, but it 'probly wasn't an apple."

"Y-You mean to tell me a ghost visited you two; and what do you mean it wasn't an apple?"

"Yep, that's what we're saying, exactly." Etta Mae said.

"*Damn!* Now I know y'all's crazy."

"Well….Chick-a-dee, I wouldn't call us crazy, because it really did happen." Tonika said.

"At whose house did you say? 'Cause, I *want* to know, so I can make sure I don't take my black butt over there!"

"But if you think about it Stephanie, it's not that unusual." Tonika said. "The spirit realm is all around us; even now."

She had reconciled herself to the conclusion that nothing in today's world was too far-fetched.

"Well, if you say so, Tonika. Anything is possible, I-I guess."

Understandably, Stephanie was still not convinced, so Tonika tried another ploy.

"Think about it! Paranormal activity is accepted as a common occurrence now. What's preventing anything from coming through opened portals?"

"Stop playing fool, this crap y'all talking ain't funny." Stephanie adamantly stated. "I haven't called up *no-body*, and I don't want to see no-body! Understand?"

"Well, I didn't call up *any*-body either, but she came. What's the world coming to?"

Etta Mae was dumbfounded by what she was hearing. It would appear Tonika was more adept in the matter of the supernatural than she'd first imagined.

Stephanie mulled the context of the conversation over in her mind. Etta Mae initially offered up her conclusion.

"You know, Mrs. Porter's dilemma reminds me of the story of Joseph."

"Who?" Stephanie and Tonika asked jointly.

"*Joseph!* You know, Israel's son.

Abraham, Isaac, and Jacob! Remember?"

Etta Mae looked at the two women expectedly, only to be met with blank stares.

"In the book of Genesis, *ladies*; the Old Testament?"

Blank faces continued to stare back at her, so she went on to explain the story. "I swear!

Joseph was a young boy whose idiot brothers had sold him to a traveling band of Ishmaelite. And it was all because of jealousy; now do you remember?"

"*Ahh!*" Etta Mae threw up both hands in exasperation. "Golly, you two need Jesus!"

117

"O, yeah! Tonika winked at Stephanie then said. "Now, I remember... in fact, I was just reading about it the other night."

"I'm sure you were Tonika." Etta Mae knowingly joked.

"I'm not lying, Etta Mae! You said Genesis, right. It's just that maybe I didn't get as far as I would've cared to, but..."

Etta Mae's face alerted Tonika that her explanation was pointless.

"I know you don't believe me, but go ahead; I know you're going to tell us all about it anyways." Tonika then said to Stephanie.

"You'd better listen closely Stephanie to what you hear, because believe me, you will see it again."

"Well... As the story goes, it seemed that Potiphar, the Pharaoh's right hand man had a wife like Mrs. Porter. Who had everything she'd wanted, except the attention of her husband, you understand. She'd lie around all day just watching poor Joseph as he went about his daily duties. Just drooling and lusting after him."

"Loungers always seem to get in trouble. You know what they say... An idle mind is certainly the devil's workshop!" Stephanie added.

"Yea, you could say that, but in the old girl's defense, Joseph *was* good on the eyes, and was exceptionally good at what he did. You feel me?"

"We feel you...Right, Stephanie?"

Stephanie's attention was now distracted by a honking horn coming from a white Cordova whose driver she recognized.

"Huh, what'd you say?"

She turned her attention once again to the street this time waving to some co-workers.

"She's not listening... Her mind is about as long as that 'scalped hair-do she's sporting."

Etta Mae snapped her fingers in the clueless face.

"Stephanie! Stay with us!"

"Stop it Etta Mae!" Tonika said laughing. "Since when did you become so devious?"

"Well, it's true!"

"O! You were saying something about a Joseph." Stephanie said.

118

"I was saying, my man Joe ran the place, while Potiphar was off doing his thing."

"Can I tell you, Potiphar trusted Joseph with everything? Everything; except his wife that is." They all broke into hysterics.

"Well… One day Sistah-Girl got Joseph in so much trouble… all because she couldn't control herself!"

"You know what y'all? it is sure enough hot as you know what out here!" Stephanie said. "I'm dying to hear the outcome of your story, but why don't we just finish this little tale inside the mall where it's cooler. Okay? Heck, my bus just left anyways."

She picked up her bags and headed toward the mall entrance without bothering to see if the ladies were following. They were of course, but not without muttering a few expletives.

A blast of cold air engulfed them with a welcoming relief from the stifling heat outside when the automatic doors opened.

They quickly made their way to the nearest bench, as their tired feet were yelling for the much needed reprieve.

"Whew! That's much better." Stephanie said.

The mall was surprisingly empty for a Saturday evening. It looked almost as if they'd walked into a "Twilight Zone."

"It's a full parking lot, but where'd all the people go?" Stephanie wondered.

Suddenly over the air waves, they heard a familiar song, 'The Look of Love is in your eyes….'"

The women closed their eyes and swayed to the melodious tune as sweet days gone by flooded their minds.

"OMG! Y'all, Look!"

Something most unusual had happened. An incarnated apparition stood before them.

"Uh, ladies, this is so *weird!*"

"O, no!" Tonika yelled. "They're following us!"

"Who are they?" Stephanie asked. "Why is she dressed like its Halloween in this weather?"

119

Tonika made an attempt to explain what was happening to the frightened skeptic.

"That, my friend, apparently is Mrs. Potiphar. It looks as though we can't get away from them!"

"Miss Who?" Stephanie asked while reaching for her bags. "Are you fools crazy? Ghosts have been visiting you all day, and you two are acting like its normal!"

"What else can you do?" Etta Mae remarked.

"I don't know, but I'm getting out of here; and away from you two loonies!"

"*Oh*, girl, now just hold on." Etta Mae said. She threw out her arm to restrain the frightened damsel's flight.

"It's all good, they're harmless enough. At least this way you're getting to hear the Bible first hand."

"You sure are." Tonika added. "This is the Bible, *walking* and *talking!*"

"Mrs. Potiphar was a sight to behold as an Egyptian royalty. The transposed figure was dressed in a gold satin body-hugging, floor length gown that ended in at least a foot of train.

A bejeweled serpent head-dress adorned the braided jet black hair. Eyelids embellished with dark shades of purple dramatized a flawless oval face.

The fixed piercing eyes were lined with the thickest of black char-coal.

The finely chiseled nose with narrowed nostrils sat above pouting lips, seemingly as ripe, and as swollen as a newly picked pomegranate. Elongated ornate gold pear shaped earrings, ending in small blossoms of flowers dangled from delicate pierced ears.

The three mesmerized women nervously watched as she approached them.

"*Humph*" She uttered, in a raspy seductive voice. "*I don't know what Joseph was talking about! I know I had it going on. When he thought I wasn't looking, I caught him watching me out of the corner of his eye. He pretended he wasn't interested in what I had to offer, but, as you can see, I knew better!*"

Beautiful hands slid seductively over a curvaceous figure.

"After all, who could keep their eyes off of all this? And besides … I'm working this dress!"

"Oh, no she didn't!" Stephanie defiantly said. "Did you hear that?"Who could keep their eyes off all this?" Now, ain't she something?"

"I take it, women were full of themselves even back then." Tonika said.

"Ladies! Don't try to comprehend it all just yet, but just listen and learn… Listen and learn!" Etta Mae said.

The annoyed specter paced the floor. The swishing sound generated by the movement of the elaborate gown echoed through the empty corridors of the mall.

"Well…If you're all finished!"

She bellowed at the ladies. The three chatty observers became motionless. Mrs. Potiphar started in on her saga once again.

"Thank you! … Now as it turns out old Joseph could!"

"Could what?" Tonika questioned. "I'm sorry, but I forgot what you'd said before."

"Keep his hands off of all that!" Etta Mae reiterated. Mrs. Potiphar waited patiently with her hands on her hips. Then she began.

"You see, it went something like this;"My plan was to take our master/ servant relationship a little further. I'd given the household servants the day off, and called my boy Joseph into the house. Then I proceeded to put the squeeze on him. But look here, I'd gotten so far as to grab him, but all it got me was a hand full of coat!"

"Now I know who you are." Stephanie declared. "All those years in Sunday School as a child have finally paid off. But I have one question to ask you."

"You have a question for me?"

"Yes mam!"

"Well, pray tell. What is your question?"

"Why were you grabbing all up on that man? And it certainly wasn't your *'prerogative,'*because 'Women's Lib' was nowhere to be found! Now am I right ladies?"

"You're right." Etta Mae agreed.

"You got that right! That's what we call sexual harassment in these days and times!" Tonika said.

"Why do you think in deed?" Mrs. Potiphar said, countering with her own question.

"It wasn't enough I was made to feel inferior in my day …. But today too? If you ask me, the whole fiasco has been over played."

"I don't know why you would say something like that; we're talking about a man's life." Etta Mae said. "How do you justify your actions?"

"How? Do you really want to know?"

"Yes!" They all shouted.

"Simply because there's no doubt in my mind, female slaves were made available for my husband, so I figured a male slave should've been available for me."

"Oh, you did, did you?" Tonika said.

"Oh, and did I mention he was easy on the eyes? And besides the fact, my husband was seemingly always gone!"

"So what you're basically saying, is that your husband was gone a lot, but he wasn't really gone."

Stephanie eyed the materialized apparition through narrowed-eyelids.

"And if I understand you correctly, Joseph supposedly got into all that trouble because your 'Love Muffin' was missing in action?"

"My Love Muffin, what's this muffin thing?"

"Your husband, dear. And poor Joseph, the poor thing didn't see the light of day for years!"

"Well if that's what you read, but it wasn't my fault."

Stephanie's spirit rose up in anger behind the snug smirk on Mrs. Potiphar's face.

"Now ain't that a blip! Well, whose fault was it then?"

She felt the need to defend Joseph's honor against the conniving spirit.

"It sure wasn't Joseph's! It wasn't his fault old Mr. 'P' couldn't take care of business!"

"You go girl! You're on a roll." Tonika said encouragingly. Etta Mae looked on in total silence.

"Oh, that's nothing." Tonika intervened."That crap still happens today! I know you heard about the man who surprised his wife and her lover in his truck.

The woman realized she'd been caught red handed, cried rape. The husband shot the dude. *Bang!* Killed the man dead! And that wasn't too long ago either. You remember, Etta Mae?"

Etta Mae shook her head in acknowledgement.

Mrs. Potiphar lashed out, unable to withstand the constant barrage of insults and interruptions.

"Ladies please!" Give me a break! It's not as if it was something I did all the time!"

The women fell silent once again, startled at the sudden outburst.

"It was... Well it was just that Joseph was such a fine specimen of a man; handsome, intelligent, shrewd, and a born leader. Not to mention having his God's special favor."

Etta Mae's head shook in agreement, along with Stephanie and Tonika.

"You may be right about that, but go on tell your story! Etta Mae said.

"There he was day in and day out, with rippling muscles;always there for me to see. I bet it would've been hard for even you three not to have been enticed. You do know that 'Mother Nature's' raging fires burn brightly on her own don't you?"

Etta Mae couldn't refrain from commenting.

"Yes, they do, but we have our own fireman to put out our fires. Well... At least I do."

Pleased with themselves on Etta Mae's comeback, the ladies slapped high fives.

"Ohhh! What are you three imbeciles saying? In case you didn't know it, my slaves were there to do my every whim! When I clapped my hands, they jumped. And dare I say, how high! I'm not used to being denied anything!"

"There, there; easy now Miss 'P' don't go getting your panties in a bunch. We didn't mean to upset—

"Panties in a bunch!" Stephanie was overcome with laughter once again.

"Now that's a good one. Did you even wear panties?"

Etta Mae and Tonika merely chuckled.

The Egyptian specter didn't know what to make of such a barbaric display of humor. Surely these women understood her plight.

"Didn't that one with the hair pulled back in a ponytail so tight, her eyes slanted, just make a reference to the same thing happening to someone a few days ago? Why then do they find my tale so overwhelming?" She wondered.

"You ladies just don't seem to understand! Joseph wouldn't submit to me, a-and I just lost it! That man was so sure of himself!"

"Sistah Girl," Etta Mae could keep silent no longer, she'd had enough.

"What you didn't know was that Joseph was only being true to his God, as well as showing his gratitude to your husband.

And besides, you knew for yourself that 'Joe' had the run of the place. So, don't even trip!"

Now all three women are on the attack. Stephanie, with a braver demeanor, walked up to the spirit.

"So tell me Miss 'Lust Bunny,' what did Joseph do after you cornered him?"

"What do you think he did? You supposedly read the story in what you call your Sunday School."

Not one to back down from a confrontation, Mrs. Potiphar stood toe to toe with the short cropped-hair tyrant.

"I told you…He took off like a bat out of hell; left coat behind and ego too!"

"And if I remember correctly that's when you framed him, you old Jezebel!" I swear I feel about you, just about how I feel about that Eve!" Tonika bellowed.

"Who are you calling a Jezebel? Who… and what's that suppose to mean? You don't know me! You may think you do, but you don't!"

"Oh, don't worry yourself too much, honey, that was long after your reign, and believe me, you're better off not knowing!" Etta Mae pointedly stated. "But you do bear a striking resemblance in character to old 'Jezzie' though. You're both conniving."

"Now, I don't mind talking with this shorter one." Mrs. Photiphar thought to herself.

"*She carries herself much better than the other two. A passive demeanor is much more pleasing than an aggressive one. Mental note to self; 'take a chill pill' every once and awhile.*"

She proceeded to answer the posed question.

"*To answer your question… It was just that I got to thinking. I didn't want to mess up what I'd had… I mean, I did have it good, with all the luxuries and trappings a woman could want. So I figured I had better protect myself just in case Joseph decided he'd wanted to squeal.*"

She addressed this to Etta Mae, more so than to the others.

"*I couldn't have that. He was such a loyal and faithful servant to his master, so I beat him to the punch!*

After all, I still had his coat as proof. So, when as you say, Mr. 'P' got home, I told him his best servant, his most loyal Hebrew slave had tried to seduce me."

"Just lied through your teeth!" Stephanie shouted. "And I bet you weren't a bit ashamed. Now, were you?"

"*Nope*, Mrs. Potiphar brazenly replied. "*I can't say that I was! Honey, I was saving my own neck. Plus, I needed to show Joseph you don't deny Mrs. Potiphar anything, and get away with it!*"

And Potiphar, just like a big dummy fell for your lie?" Stephanie asked.

"*Hook, line and sinker, as you say! The man was livid, to say the least. "To the dungeon with you!" He'd yelled. "What; the dungeon? So I thought… Now, wait a minute that was supposed to cost Joseph his head.*

She stepped away head lowered.

"*But, what it really told me was that my husband actually believed in his slave more than he did me.*"

"Aha!…So it turned out, he wasn't as dumb as you thought."

Tonika couldn't help but comment after listening quietly for a change.

"*No, apparently not. It seemed he couldn't kill a man he knew in his heart was innocent. But due to his pride, and his reputation, he had to punish the once-valued slave in some way. And as fate would have it, Joseph, as you know, became even greater in prison, interpreting dreams and all.*"

"Yay! Way to go Joe!"

The ladies clapped and cheered on Joseph's behalf.

"Yaa-aay! I for one am just glad your husband saw through your big lie, and didn't hurt that poor innocent man!" Tonika added.

"Miss 'P' you couldn't have known it at the time, but God was going to use your boy Joseph in a mighty way. And Joseph said it himself, and I paraphrase;"What the devil meant for bad, God used it for His good, to save many lives."

And another thing, it wasn't Pot's doing either. It was divine providence! Joseph was going to save those brothers of his, along with a whole nation. The PP & B were just humbling assignments for God's servant. So don't go beating yourself up about it too much, okay."

"You think so Etta Mae ... but what's this PP & B?"

"I'm sorry, but PP&B stands for the pit, the palace, and the brothers. Oh, and I forgot one, the prison."

"Now, I see; I didn't know."

The grand dame had been truly touched by her favorite human's words. Unlike the other two she devils, the kind woman had cared enough to extend the olive branch.

"Well, that makes me feel better, but ladies things were never the same between my husband and me after that. He never trusted me again."

"Oh boo, hoo, hoo, what a shame. And after all you went through."

Mrs. Potiphar turned to personally address the antagonizing being.

"Stephanie, I believe? Has anyone ever lost their trust in you?"

"No... I can't think of anyone."

The twice divorcee was actually in denial about her own marital state, but she wasn't about to give this transposed apparition the pleasure of identifying with her plight.

"No? Or do you choose not to say?"

Stephanie did not acknowledge the question. The all-knowing spirit allowed the woman's lie to stand.

"Then you should be so lucky. To tell you the truth, I'm not behind bars so to speak, but I am in a prison, a prison without walls. I'm a prisoner of my own mind, and of my own doing."

She turned to walk away, still muttering under her breath.

"I'm still kicking myself! Good day ladies!"

Mrs. Potiphar seemingly faded into thin air. The three women sat entranced. Stephanie was the first to speak.

"I don't feel sorry for her. I'm glad Mr. 'P' handled his business. And I wouldn't trust the ole heifer either!" The agitated vixen continued.

"She didn't need to kick herself."

Stephanie shadow kicked the air.

"Boy, I tell you, we sure are some kicking fools today."

Tonika simply had to laugh when she saw Etta Mae's facial gesture and heard her response.

"I feel sorry for the woman, she looked so sad."

The ladies all agreed and discussed it among themselves. Then as if awakening from a dream, they all stared at each other and turned to survey their surroundings.

Familiar sounds once again filled the air. They heard the laughter of giggling teenagers walking past, engrossed in last night's shenanigans.

"W-what just happened here?"

Stephanie asked in disbelief. "Oh, that was too spooky!"

She looked to her friends for some sort of explanation.

"Now correct me if I'm wrong, but this mall was empty just a moment ago. A-and we were just talking to a Mizz-Mrs. Poti-phar, right?"

"Yes, that is correct; I warned you in the parking lot." Tonika said.

"You know what, y'all... I'm out of here."

Stephanie reached down and gathered her many bags, and made for the nearest exit. Etta Mae and Tonika stared after her.

"Bye, Stephanie!" The deserted women yelled.

"And we do have to talk!" Tonika yelled. "I'll call you!"

The automatic glass doors closed with a resounding swish behind the hastily retreating woman. She felt as if she'd been in a time warp. Stephanie reasoned any future association with the likes of Etta Mae Smith and Tonika Gibbons would be far and in between.

The eerie karma surrounding those two were too supernaturally charged for her taste. Never, she reasoned in all her thirty something years had she ever encountered the likes of what she'd just experienced.

Tonika will just have to find another source of information of her husband's exploits, but not from Stephanie Nicole Willis. Fortunately, her bus rounded the corner just at that time.

Tonika looked longingly after the one source she thought could fill in the gap surrounding the 'who' and the 'why' that was responsible for turning her world upside down, depart. She turned her attention to Etta Mae, who'd been watching her changing demeanor.

CHAPTER
Fourteen

....

"Sorry dude, but we haven't even been properly introduced, Donnie said. "Hello, I'm Donnie... Donnie LeRoy Smith, Etta Mae's husband. You know... Dee's oldest sister."

"And I just barged into your home like a charging bull, and didn't properly introduce myself. So please forgive me. Hi, I'm Damien... Damien Darnell Whitman, but my friends call me D.D."

"Double 'D,' now that wouldn't happen to stand for double-dipping now would it? *Ha, ha, ha!*"

"*Double-dipping?*" He repeated loudly. "Now why the heck would you say something like that?"

The silly statement irritated Damien so much that he responded by shoving Donnie backwards.

"Easy now, big fellow; you don't want to do that." Donnie steadied himself.

"Dee-Dee!" He said laughing under his breath.

"What is so damn funny?"

"Ah ... you are my good man."

"Look dude, I'm alright with whatever you call me. I know who I am, and you can bank on that."

The robust house guest shadow boxed the air. Finally, he dropped his hands to his side and stepped toward Donnie, who by then feeling a little intimidated backed further into the room.

"I've gotten in a few scrapes behind my name, you know, but I'm telling you; those very same fools had to back up off me!"

"I'm sure they did," Donnie quipped.

"You see this scar right here?" Damien pointed to a scar above his brow.

"I got that when I was in college, but you should see the other guy!"

"Bro, I'm sure you left your mark alright. What did you do slap him?"

He slapped the air with his hands in an effeminate gesture and playfully mimicked.

"Stop it now… Quit it!"

"You're so funny."

The irony of the pun was not wasted on Damien.

"No, you're wrong; I'm not the funny one here!"

Whereas the host enjoyed making light of his guest's uneasiness, Damien, on the other hand, pursued in his quest to show case his masculinity.

"Let's just say, I had the last laugh after it was over and done, because I represented. You know what I mean?"

"I bet you represented alright! And from what I hear …. Donnie smirked. "Let's just say… Women, they do talk."

"When I said that I represented, I represented, just like I'm about to do right now!"

Damien threw sucker punches as he approached the annoying host, who in turn threw up his arm in defense.

Okay, okay, back up Brotha' Man and loosen your Speedos."

"You want some of this?"

"No dude, I'm just joking with you. And besides, you're right, I *don't* know you that well. I was just repeating what I thought I picked up from our wives conversation.

"Oh… So I get it; Delilah's been having diarrhea of the mouth!"

Damien looked inquiringly at his host. He finally understood his plight. He walked over to the couch and sat down.

"You might say that." Donnie said as he took the seat across from his now solemn guest. Instinct said the two were about to charter dangerous waters.

"Well, I wouldn't go jumping to any conclusions, if I were you." Damien said in his own defense. "There are always two sides to every story. It's what you might say, curiosity can and does get the best of you. Plus the fact, one has to keep one's options open."

Damien stood and flexed his muscles. "You know what I mean?"

"Uh, huh."

"Just how much has Delilah told her sister?" Damien asked.

"Well to be frank, Dee hasn't really said that much, not even to Etta Mae, but it was more like what she didn't say."

"Oh, so now you're a psychic on top of being a class ass jerk!"

"If that's what you want to call it. Look, I have to tell you, your girl's pretty pissed off, okay. So I'm just deducing what I think it is."

"You deduce?"

"As a matter of fact you don't have to be a rocket scientist, to know what you closeted brothers are into these days. You can read any magazine and know what time it is."

Donnie kept silent about the conversation he had earlier with his sister-in-law.

"Oh, so you're up on all the latest, huh? Do explain yourself further… please sir."

"Man; listen. When women get to a place where they can't talk about something then you can take it to the bank that it's something too deep for their psyche to grasp!"

"Fool, you're tripping."

"Tripping, or not… but needless to say, that's what led to my conclusion."

"I can't believe you, dude."

"You're a brother on the 'DL.' Now, you have to admit… *that's deep!*"

"So that's how you came up with it, huh?"

Damien stood with one hand cupped beneath his chin.

"And in all your deducing you came up with I'm on the D L."

"Yep, that's my story and I'm sticking to it."

"Humph!" Damien muttered, without acknowledging the irritating nuisance accuracy.

"And I tell you something else I read about you dudes in Schwarz—
He stopped as in thought.

"Uh, oh, now I'm sounding like my wife."

Damien was reminded of a conversation between him and Delilah.

"I'm sure Delilah read that article too. She commented on it at dinner last Thursday."

"I bet that made your old butt squirm." Donnie laughed.

"Let's just say I'm lucky she didn't see the look on my face. And I might add it also helped that my back was turned."

"I just don't see what's so good about all this deception going on with our people."

"Who's deceiving whom?"

"Are you kidding me?"

"Look, I have to say that I have no regrets."

Damien chose not to acknowledge the disdainful look directed his way, but continued on with his statement.

"Life *can* get pretty boring. Besides, it's not like it hasn't been going on for years."

"I feel sorry for you, my dear man." Donnie finally said. "You're wrong and you'll have to speak for yourself on that one!"

"Please don't pity me, kind sir."

"I'm just glad that crap wasn't going on when I was your age."

"Are you serious?"

"Yes, I'm as serious as a heart attack. You young people are something else these days!"

"*Dude!*" Damien shouted. "What world do you live in?"

"Why, the same one as you, of course!"

"Don't be so sure." Damien countered. "Maybe it's only because Schwarz didn't have the guts to print anything like that back then! You know there's nothing new under the sun, and you can bank on that!"

"Yeah, yeah, if you say so, man."

"I can bet you there were plenty of skeletons rattling around in some closets in your day as well!"

"Hmmm, on second thought, you know you could be right." Donnie admitted. "I'm sure this wasn't just invented, but I thank God I was never privy to know anyone."

Damien was at a loss for words, after he heard what Donnie had to say.

"And I mean that! Black folks didn't tolerate that sort of stuff back when I was a boy."

"Huh! You wish they didn't. You were just too naïve, that's all that was."

Damien defiantly folded his arms.

"Come to think of it, now that you mention it. I used to wonder about Deacon George Gray. He was kind 'a strange, now that I think on it. Umph!"

"And did he have a wife?" Damien asked.

"Yep, he sure did; Sister Ramona Gray."

"You see! And not only in the church, but you probably rubbed shoulders with a few in the locker room too, and didn't know it."

Damien felt much calmer now that he could openly discuss the matter.

"And did you ever get slapped on the butt with a towel after you showered in the gym?" He asked. "If so, I just hope you didn't drop the soap!"

"Do I look like a fool? Let's just say, I didn't bend over to pick it up. I won't about to give those fools any kind of reason to play a prank on me like that."

"It would've served you right, if you ask me!"

"Not around those crazy guys! I already told you, Mama didn't raise no fool! If I dropped it, it stayed dropped."

The tension between the two was beginning to dissipate as Donnie continued.

"Those fools were always acting crazy. You never knew what they would do next. I wasn't about to give play to the devil!"

"I know what you mean; some of my best fights were in the locker room. Damn that Fred Tomkins!"

"I don't know about you, but if I wrote a book on the exploits of my life, I'd probably end up with a best seller."

He reclined in the chair and interlocked his hands behind his head.

"No, please allow me to be the first." said Damien. "I should write one starting with my childhood."

"Shucks, who needs to write a book, all you have to do is let a woman get a whiff of your secrets and then it's on!" Donnie said. "The phones would be ringing off the hook, with "Girl, did you hear?""

"And not only that! By the time they finished adding to it, your life could be made into the movie of the week!"

Raucous laughter erupted between the two.

"Yeah, and you know they'd have to spice it up and make it even juicier than what it actually was." Damien added.

"Etta Mae and Tonika would have a field day with it. And get this, they would find something in the 'Bible to relate it to. At least my wife would."

Ding dong.

The sound of the doorbell caused Donnie's muscles to tense. He bolted upright from his reclined position. The thought of who it could be held him motionless.

"Here we go again! Now who could this be?"

Looking to the befuddled house guest but not really expecting an answer Donnie rises.

"Damn! It's Grand Central Station around here today."

Donnie opened the door to find a gangly dreadlock wearing teenager standing before him with a container filled with items to sell.

"Good afternoon sir; I'm from 'GITYO,' the 'Get It Together Youth Organization.' I was wondering if you'd be interested in buying an item or items to help support our mission. The mission is to keep youth like myself out of trouble, by providing a stable environment. The proceeds help support a summer camp for youth like me."

The young man read from an embossed card he was holding.

"Ooh man, you didn't even bother to breathe while you read all that. I'm impressed." Donnie lightheartedly said. "I know you're nervous, I would be too."

"No sir." The young man answered.

"GITYO? Does that stand for, Gityo' act together?"

"No sir."

"Uh um… okay then… you're a man of few words I see. What you got in there?"

"Candy bars, batteries, carwash chamois… and some other stuff."

"And some other stuff." Donnie mocked. "Okay man, I'll help you out. Anything to keep you young people on the up and up."

"Yes sir, I mean, thank you."

"Let me have two of those chocolate candy bars.

He handed the young man a five spot.

"Keep the change, my good man."

The young man stood in anticipation.

"Ah, sir… a-actually, I need another five dollars from you, p-please."

"What? You mean to tell me these candy bars are five dollars apiece?"

Yes sir, t-they are."

The young man nervously adjusted the waste of his pants while he waited for the miser to fish into his pockets for another five spot.

"Here you go… you got me on this one."

"Thank you sir, have a fantastic day."

"And you do the same."

Donnie closed the door and approached Damien. He held the bars of candy as if they were bars of gold.

"Here, you care for one?"

He handed a candy bar to his by now, famished house guest.

"Sure, thanks."

They quickly tore into the wrappers, and gobbled down the sweet delectable in two bites.

"Oh man that hit the spot. I've got a good mind to tackle my wife's chicken salad, but I want to see tomorrow."

"Go eat that sandwich you made." Damien said. "I'm sure that big fly left you some."

"As far as I'm concerned, he could've taken it with him."

The men shared a much needed laugh.

"Etta Mae had better not be spending my raise either, while she's at the mall. I knew it was a mistake telling her."

"Ah, yes, that's a big mistake, a big no, no. Dude, a man never, ever, ever, let a woman in on all his financial holdings. *Some*; never all."

"I know, you're right about that. You should've seen those beautiful, brown eyes light up!"

"Now I know your wife and mine are true sisters."

"Oh, money trouble on the old home front, aye?"

"No. I don't really mind what she spends. She backs her car out of the drive the same as me. Besides, I take my stress out on the golf course, so it's all good."

"You sure appear to put a lot of value on your golfing. Now you see how a man's attention can get away from his home life."

"Oh, no you don't. You can't put what you do, and what I do in the same category."

All I'm saying… as much time you spend on the golf range… and look here; can any of the fella's say you're actually at the range?"

"And just what might you be implying?"

"I'm just saying…." Damien turned his back to Donnie.

"Believe me when I tell you." Donnie forcibly grabbed the instigator's arm, and spun him around to face him.

"I'm where I say I am, and Etta Mae knows it! If nothing else, my lucky golf shirt can speak for me!"

"Lucky golf shirt? What does a shirt have to do with her knowing where you are?"

"Now *think* about it." Donnie chided. "I'm out there in the hot blazing sun, walking and sweating for miles, behind this little white ball. Now, if I came home all showered and smelling fresh, don't you think she would suspect something?"

In his best Etta Mae's voice; "Why're you smelling so fresh; I thought you went golfing."

"Okay, okay, I get your point, you're right." Damien said amused.

"Humph, I know I'm right. Those ole hawk-eyes don't miss *nothing*!"

"You sure know your woman, because her sister—

"And she had the nerve to wash my shirt the other day before a big tournament. Pissed me off! Then she and ole motor-mouth had a laugh about it."

"What?" Not the infamous golf shirt!" Damien said laughing.

"I'm telling you man, I was as mad as a hornet knocked out of his nest!"

Just thinking about it caused Donnie to pace the floor.

"Say man, you do wash your shirt don't you?" Damien asked wrinkling his nose.

"To answer your question; no. No, I don't, all my karma might be washed out of it."

Donnie allowed his mind to reflect on his last golf outing.

"Call me superstitious if you want."

"Oh, I'm sure you and that shirt are pleasant to be around."

Damien held his nose again.

"Yeah, yeah, you're so funny." Donnie said. "Let's get back to why you're here. Let me ask you this, does the name Alma Wallington mean anything to you?"

"Yes, I've heard of her." Damien answered. "She's that black author, and her book's called, 'Erica Bags a Fledgling.' Why? It's been years since her fiasco of a marriage came to the forefront.

"Good, then you do know what went down with her."

"What made you bring her up?"

"Oh, no reason other than to say your marriage identifies with hers."

Damien set his mind on the task at hand. He sensed the man across from him really wasn't done with the matter of his life.

"Did you ever stop to think about the situation she found herself in?"

"No, and just what are you getting at?"

Damien fidgeted with one of the two multi-colored Phoenician glass rabbits that sat on the coffee table.

"Am I correct in saying it was a bunch of mess, kind sir?" Donnie inquired in his mock Englishman voice.

"Yes, it was, and I'm sorry to say that mental telepathy of yours has paid off. "Damn it to hell!"

Distraught, Damien rose to his feet and walked away with clench fists stuffed deeply in his pant pockets.

"I did hear that she was coping with it pretty well though."

"She said she didn't intend to be a victim any longer. Perhaps that's what my sissy-n-law is thinking too!"

"Don't count on it; I'm not going to give up that easily!"

"And I wouldn't go getting any big ideas either if I were you!"

Donnie said with a smug look on his face. "From the looks of it brother, I think your butt's going to go through the ringer!"

"Anyone ever tell you that with a friend like you who needs an enemy?"

"Say what you want but I know Alma's not alone in this. There're other forsaken women going through the very same hell."

Donnie would not allow himself to fall prey to the discomfort his guest was experiencing.

"You sorry brothers ought a' be ashamed of yourselves!"

"I tell you what amazes me." Damien said.

"And what would that be kind sir?"

"How you are all up in my damn business! And I wish you would quit it with the brothers like you crap! Damn it! You're a brother too in case you haven't noticed!"

"Yes, you're right!" Donnie adamantly responded. And I'm all brotha' make no mistake about it! Everything's normal about this! Old 'Hank' serves his purpose well, the way he was meant to."

Donnie glanced down at his lower parts.

"With a woman! Now you can bank on that! Hank is definitely not confused what garage he parks in…just ask my wife!"

"Ask my wife, ask my wife this ask my wife that!" Damien muttered under his breath.

The wavered host heard but didn't bother to respond to the man's sarcasm.

"And I'm sure your wife has a tale of woes on how, Hank can't park in the garage anymore because of oil leaks."

"You're full of bull!"

Damien's remark had finally struck a sore cord with the agitated host.

"Believe me; you don't want to go there!"

"Slow your road dude! I was just saying. I am sorry to hear that Delilah is upset. I guess I was just hoping; she could understand that's all."

"Fool, you're asking a lot out of that poor woman!" Donnie walked away."And you hope she understands."

"Yes, I said I hope she can understand."

"There ain't that much understanding in the world! It's not like you stepped out with another woman, dude. You cheated with someone with the same equipment as you!"

"Now if that's not a slap in the old girl's face, I don't know what is!"

Damien stood there absorbing it all. He wasn't thinking too respectful of this sinister man at the moment.

The irritating 'Don E. Do-Right's constant reminder of how dire the situation he faced was beginning to fray his nerves.

"Who did he think he was anyway? And besides, my father used to say that we all fall short of the glory... So this dude needs to get off his glory-horse and come down to where the brothers walk."

"*Hello!* Are you with me, or have you traveled elsewhere?" Donnie snapped his fingers in Damien's face.

"In case you didn't know it, it's not okay to cheat with another woman either. For all I know, you could've dipped your stick—

Donnie's gasp almost depleted the air supply in the room. The look of astonishment on the offended man's face made it necessary for Damien to change the subject.

"Uh, mm, sounds like you have a great wife, if she is anything like Delilah...."

"Don't insult me, I wouldn't dare!" Donnie said in a barely audible tight voice.

"Unlike you wimps of today, I took my wedding vows serious when I got married, and I still do!"

"Sorry partner, I didn't know what I said was going to cause such a stir."

The priest of his domain was not willing to admit that he'd once come close to having a fling some years ago with a clerk at the country club. He recognized that experience as being at his weakest moment.

"Nope, Etta Mae's the only girl for me. And I can't say that the two sisters are anything alike, thank God. More like night and day, oil and water—

"Okay, okay I get the point... geez!"

Damien lifted his hands in surrender to curtail the verbal barrage.

"But here's something for you to ponder, maybe you're not replacing her with another woman, but what about that little white ball you run after every chance you get? Huh?"

"I just told you that Etta Mae and Dee are like day and night, and I don't need to be all up under my wife every time she turns around!"

"Humph! If you say so, but I'll make it up to Delilah one way or other."

"I don't know man, you'll have to bend over backwards to make this one up!"

Donnie laughed in total abandonment.

"Oops, no pun intended big fella."

"There you go again! You just can't be serious, can you? And why are you so concerned with my sexual exploits?"

"I'm not concerned for my sake, but when it affects what's close to me..."

Well, if you ask me—

"To change the subject, I wouldn't count on Dee loving you that much. 'Cause look here, there's some things a woman just won't stand for! And I think you've hit the mother lode! Course now, I could be wrong.

"That's right, you'll wrong."

"It does look as if you fella's can get away with anything these days, and your women will stick like glue."

"Such as?"

Damien thought he might have found a ray of hope in what his 'know it all in-law' said. Just then the telephone rang. Donnie lifted the receiver.

"H-hello... *Oh!* Cynthia... how're you baby girl? I-we're doing good. Yes, uh huh... well good to hear. Uh huh, I hope you had a fabulous time in the Five-O state. Me and Etta plan to make it over there real soon. Come to think of it, we have an anniversary coming up. Huh? No your sister's not here; she and our neighbor left early today for shopping. You know your sister and her shopping. *Ha, ha, ha...* I know that's right. She did get it honest. O-okay, yeah call her on her cell... maybe she'll hear it. *Ha, ha, ha.* Okay, baby, you take care, and we'll be talking with ya' soon, okay. Uh huh... love you too, bye-bye now."

"That was Cynthia looking for Etta Mae. And you noticed I didn't say anything about you or Dee."

"Yes, I noticed... and I don't know whether it was good or bad."

"Well, I figured if you wanted her to know anything, Etta Mae would tell her. *Ha, ha, ha!*"

"I'm sure you're right about that. Now you were saying something about a wife sticking with..."

"Oh yeah, I meant men are doing some stupid stuff! Just last week this well known philanthropist, photographed his 'atta boy', and sent it to a friend via the web. The only thing is...it ended up all over MyTube. Now wasn't that something?"

"I must say, that was pretty darn hilarious! *Ha, ha, ha!* Another victim falls prey to the old 'social media' highway. Your business is not all your business, because it will become everyone else's business!"

"You're right, nothing safe." Damien said.

"But the thing is... can you believe his wife is going to stick by him? It's no different than the infamous "I did not have sex with that woman.""

Damien hoped to God that the same strength those women found to forgive their spouses, his wife would do likewise. He didn't exactly know why it was so crucial for Delilah forgive him.

His brain couldn't seem to comprehend it. It was as if he wasn't acting on his own accord. Why had he run after her, when clearly their union was over? In any case, through no will of his own, he'd cast the bread on the water, and maybe, just maybe, the baited fish would snap it up.

"You know, uh, I mean, I know." Damien interjected. "My wife does love me. I just hope she loves me that much. She knows I'm the best thing that's ever happened to her.

Plus, she's not exactly a 'spring chicken,' now you do know that! Not to mention that she's been around the block a time or two."

"So…What're you doing now, trying to justify why she should take you back, by belittling her?"

"I'm just saying! There are quite a few notches under the old girl's belt. Let's see… what am I? Oh yes, number six!"

"Now you see, the moment I start to feel sorry for your bug-ass, you open your mouth and say something dumb.

The woman looks damn good for her age, and I'm sure you didn't turn down any blessings!"

Donnie took a stand in his absent sister-in-laws defense.

"It's not like you think."

"Not like I think? Oh, and are you trying to say that her money didn't have anything to do with you marrying her? Negro, please! And I say that loosely!"

"Are you kidding me? I don't need any of Delilah's money!" Damien said, appalled at the insinuation. "Lord knows, I've worked too long and too hard to become somebody's gigolo."

"Now, remember you called yourself a gigolo' not me."

"I never said I was a saint; that's your department. But I do have my own money!"

"I'm sure you do… glad to hear it."

"You see hombre, you never know what lies in a man."

Donnie was growing weary by the minute. His favorite program had long since been off the air. And his poor sandwich…. He looked longingly at the front door, wishing the obtrusive-being would somehow find his exit.

"We better be glad those women aren't here to hear all this bull we're shooting!"

The sudden outburst startled Damien, who was also lost in a train of thought. He stole a look at his watch.

"I wonder when Delilah is going to return."

Donnie harbored the same thought and pretentiously called out "Ett-aa! Where are you?"

The strange bed-fellows couldn't help but laugh at the awkwardness of their situation.

142

"I can't stay here too much longer! I wonder when that woman is coming back." He checked his time piece once again. Donnie watched as he nervously shuffled his feet.

The room was seemingly closing in. Damien undid another button, as a trickle of sweat ran down the crevice of his sternum.

The distraught host who felt as if nothing in life was the same anymore, settled into his Lazy Boy. Here he is having this stupid conversation about men on men when all he'd wanted for the evening was a little peace and quiet.

Damien on the other hand oblivious to the thoughts the older gentleman harbored continued with his banter.

"A lot of your sisters are not what they're cracked up to be you know!"

"Look, damn it!"

Donnie, now beyond being tired, jumped up and crossed the room. And before he knew it, he'd grabbed the 'house guest from hell' by the shoulders and forcibly shook him.

"You need to stop with all this crazy chatter! I'm about sick of it! Grow up, will you!"

Damien shook loose of the iron grip, and stepped back. It appeared to him, basically, that the two of them would never see eye to eye on anything.

He'd wanted to leave, but hadn't wanted to chance missing his wife's return. But where could neutral ground be found, was the question of the moment.

Donnie left the room and went into the kitchen. The pang of hunger had become too great to ignore. The forgotten sandwich sat on the counter, beckoning with the look of hunger quenching delight.

He stood in thought. "Should I, or shouldn't I? Oh, hell! If it's good enough for that damn fly, then it's has to be good enough for me."

He took a knife out of the drawer and divided the sandwich in half. Donnie poured two glasses of ice tea and carried the meal back into the living room.

"Aha!" Damien thought. Since he wanted to go there, we could talk religion. He said this more so to annoy Donnie than anything else.

"Sorry about before, but my stomach was growling, so I broke down and decided my sandwich would become my savior. Care for some?"

"Hell yeah! Let me at it, I was about to drop from hunger."

Damien's first thought was about the fly, but his stomach growled, 'feed me, feed me,' with every passing minute. He reached for his half of the sandwich and the refreshing glass of tea.

"Mm, mm, this is good. It was either this or my wife's forbidden chicken salad."

Donnie wiped a smear of mustard from his chin.

"Un hum, un hum." Was all Damien could mutter between bites.

Before you knew it, the whole sandwich and iced tea had been consumed. One loud belch sealed their state of contentment.

"That won't bad at all, in fact, it was downright delicious." Damien said.

"That my friend was my famous 'Donnie Detonator.' Of course, it would've been much better had it not been hours old."

"It was alright by me, it well served its purpose."

"Uh oh, we forgot to say grace. Now, I know I'm glad my wife's not here."

"Now don't go getting all religious on me. What's the world coming to? Every time you turn around, people quoting Scripture… Jesus this, and Jesus that! To tell you the truth, my boy, I'm sick of it!"

"Whoa… what bought this on?" Donnie asked. "If I'd known a full stomach would've caused you to blaspheme, I'd left you to starve."

Sure enough Donnie rose to the occasion, and adamantly stated.

"Well it looks like to me you're running from something!"

"Me…running? From what, dare I ask?"

"Something say, like maybe a 'calling' perhaps?"

"Hell yeah, I've been called alright, everything but a child of God, by my wife! I hearda voice… but it sure wasn't God's!"

Damien shucked his teeth and turned away.

Donnie grabbed a nine iron from his golf bag and placed a ball on the floor. He lightly tapped and sent the ball scurrying across the room.

"Oh, she sure had grounds to!"

"She did at that." Damien stated. But you brought it up, remember? And God did make all mankind!"

"So I did… What was I thinking?" Donnie said without looking up.

"When did men become such wimps? Now just look at who caused 'my man to lose all he had." Damien went on. "A woman! A brotha' was' sitting phat! I'm telling you we men were meant to rule the world!"

Donnie looked up questionably wanting to know exactly where this was leading. He never expected this worldly man to dive so deeply into religion. He took one hand off the iron hoping to quiet the man's over exuberance.

"Bring it down a notch, will you? What's gotten into you anyway?"

"Sorry, I gota little carried away." Damien said apologetically.

"Dude you got more patches than my grandmother's quilt! First, you don't want to talk religion, now look at you. I can't shut you up!"

"Well, that's something else you don't know about me, I am a well learned man." Damien said proudly.

You trying to say you know enough to exegete the Word or to eisegete it?" A puzzled look overcame Damian's face, prompting Donnie to further explain.

"Was it what you read into it, or, was it, what you drew from it? Duhh! You understand now?"

"Okay… I didn't tell you but, I am a 'preacher's kid,' so I do know something about the Word."

"Get out of here!" Donnie exclaimed. "Do they know about their boy-eee!"

"Both my parents are deceased."

"Sorry man…that was uncalled for. I was just ribbing you a bit."

Then to get back on a lighter note, he brought up the morning's occurrences once again.

"Besides I told you weird thing's been happening around here. First Etta Mae's weird dream and then 'close encounters of the third kind', so I'd best stop talking.

I can't say who might just pop up." He glanced eerily around the room, and then playfully added. "Like you!"

"You jive turkey... you're stuffed with something... but it sure ain't cornbread!"

"I told you, and you thought I was kidding." Donnie said laughing. I watched it play out from my hiding place in the closet." He was too embarrassed to say that he had actually peed his pants in the hallway.

"You talking about somebody scared!" Donnie grabbed at his chest. "Why I thought I's going to meet my Maker."

Damien was flabbergasted and doesn't know what to make of this man and his ever changing antics.

From what little time he'd spent here Damien just couldn't figure if he was ever serious or if he merely humored him. But on this matter, to be safe he chose to disbelieve. He nervously paced the floor, challenging Donnie's words.

"I thought you were kidding, when you talked that shit earlier." Damien shakily said. "Lord what have I walked into?"

"So be careful, I told you your girl Eve's been up in here today!"

Donnie continued to weave his tale, amused at the discomfort he was witnessing.

If truth be told, ghost stories have always terrified Damien. He recalled how his grandmother and her girlfriends would sit and talk for hours how 'hants' would be in ceilings of old haunted houses. How way-farers would stop nightly to rest only to be confronted by the disembodied spirits.

It would seem to Damien, having been blessed with a vivid imagination, he himself would end up being the unfortunate traveler. He would become so engrossed in the tale-weaving that fear would grip him with an iron fist.

It hadn't help that he would have to climb dark stairs alone to sleep in a dark bedroom. The many dead bodies that he'd witnessed lain out in the sanctuary of his father's church would come to the fore front of his mind.

"Shut up, damn you!" Damien shouted feeling a cold chill run up and down his back."

"Oka-ay... Moving on...." Donnie said. He realized he had somehow actually spooked the now trembling man standing before him. "But don't say I didn't warn you."

"Look here, I know what you're trying to do, but I'm not buying it." Damien said.

"You're not buying what?" Donnie asked.

"You know what, that same bull you were talking earlier when I knocked on your door. Thinking I was the devil or some stupid mess."

"Oh well, suit yourself, Mr. I Can't Believe It's Butter!" Donnie resolved. "Doubting Thomas does not have anything on you."

"If Adam hadn't had that surgery we'd still be in that 'Garden' right now!"

Damian thought he'd initiate a previous topic to change the subject and drove home his point by stomping feet.

"Come to think of it, did he even ask God for that woman?" All this supernatural talk was getting the best of the man. "You back on that again? Didn't I say to be careful what you say?

Donnie pinches the tip of his nose when he is annoyed or in a position of uncertainty.

"And that's something you'll have to ask Etta Mae, she can tell you better than I can."

"Come, oh great A-dam."

Damian didn't fully believe anything out of the ordinary would occur, so he pressed the issue. "Come, oh great one! Ooo-ooo!"

"Fool! Would you shut up?"

Donnie's nose really got a work out as he tried unsuccessfully to shush the unbeliever.

"You think you're funny, don't you? But if you keep playing around, my man Adam just might answer your call!"

CHAPTER

Delilah's afternoon walk proved to be more challenging than she had anticipated. The hot blazing afternoon sun beat down; it seemed to her, mercilessly.

The three quarters length jacket she'd worn was moist with sweat. The purple 'V' neck tee worn beneath the gray rayon caprice ensemble clung to her back wet with moisture.

She slid the jacket off her shoulders and callously threw it across her arm. Her pace slowed as she wiped the beads of sweat from her forehead. Why had she worn these black 'croc' embossed 2" sling- back heels?

Note to self: "Think foot comfort before fashion when touring a neighborhood. She thought long and hard about the $169.00 'Ted Nardy' sneakers that lay haphazardly discarded on the bedroom floor. Oh, how she longed for their comfort.

"But no! I just had to be cute!" She chided herself but couldn't help but smile. The thought of turning around to retrieve the comfort wear crossed her mind, but decided instead to press on. It would only be a short walk anyway.

The power walker that had stepped onto the sidewalk after stretching approached her with wide determined strides.

She'd smiled, but it was actually more of a smirk when her eyes casually took in the casual stroller's inappropriate footwear.

"Hello."

The walker muttered as she side stepped the fashionable stroller to begin her jaunt. Dee returned a forced greeting.

"Hi."

She stole a glance over her shoulder in time to see the woman in full stride, tearing up the sidewalk.

Dismayed, she kicked the backless shoes off her feet hoping to ease the ache in her arch. But, the rough, hot surface beneath her feet wasn't anything she had bargained for.

"Ouch! I swear!" Dee slipped her foot into the slides once again. "I guess it's better to ache than to burn."

As she rounded a corner, blaring pulsating music accompanied by voices of rowdy revelers coming from an olive green tri-leveled house, spilled out into the street.

All makes and models of vehicles crammed the driveway. Still, hastily abandoned cars haphazardly parked lined the barely accessible street.

"Party over here, ain't bleep over there!" A raucous reveler could be heard declaring from inside. "Hoot, Hoot!" Much laughter and revelry followed the declaration.

"Humph! It sound like the party's gotten started early in there!"

Her quick reaction saved her from a rear collision with four rambunctious teenagers. Their skateboard's grinding wheels and exhilarating laughter only added to the noisy afternoon ruckus.

Dee's foot discomfort soon gave way to intrigue, as she watched a beaming young father carry a new born infant seat to an idling silver Chevrolet Suburban.

She watches how gingerly the man reaches inside smoothing the pink blanket. Once the carrier was securely locked in the rear seat, the young man went around and assisted his wife, planting a kiss on her lips as he did so.

The smiling young wife waved eagerly before she settled into the cooled air conditioned interior; thanks to her thoughtful husband. Dee returned the greeting with a hesitant wave but quickly averted her gaze.

"This place is so unlike New York City," she thought, aimlessly walking on.

After she'd awakened from her nap, Dee reasoned she needed to get out into the fresh air. She'd left the house an hour or so after her sister and friend. She hadn't cared to accompany them on their Saturday outing.

"Who wants to be a third wheel?" She thought. "It's probably something they do religiously anyway."

The jaw dropping scene she witnessed in her New York apartment was continually on rewind in her mind.

"How could he do that to me…better yet, how could he be…."

She couldn't bring herself to form the words. It almost, always stuck in her throat. "In the arms of… not another woman, but a… Man!

"There, I said it."

"You think you know a person. I thought I knew everything about Damien. I know his likes and dislikes; how he prefers dry toast as oppose to it being butter drenched."

She and her husband had, she thought a pleasurable relationship. Damien always knew where and just how to touch her. That's what was so puzzling about the whole thing.

She'd been slowly walking for some time before realizing her cheeks were wet with tears.

"Why the tears, are they from anger, or are they from the hurt and the humiliation I'm feeling?

Thank goodness, in all my marriages, I never had to embody the sheer pain that's now cutting me so deep. I was the one who chose to end each commitment."

The casual stroller distractedly plucked away at a wild dandelion blossom she'd stooped to pick.

"I guess I'll never know why it's so hard for me to form lasting relationships.

"Til death do us part," was the vow I took each time. Yet, I always walked away.

Of course, I can give myself credit for the two that left me bereft. But even then I could only mourn for a short period of time."

An unusual phenomenon occurred as she descended a sloping hill. She had become enshrouded in a cloud like haze that should have long since burned off in the smoldering heat.

Not only was she disoriented, but a blast from a honking horn, caused her to lose her footing. Dee shakily watched as the phantom car sped on its way, oblivious to her pounding heart.

The haze began to lift, and before her stood a towering white edifice. The finest of white marble marquee in the shape of a well was erected on the manicured lawn emblazoned with black onyx letters that read "**Re-dig the Wells of Jubilation Worship Center.**"

"Now that's saying a mouth full. I belong to RWJWC."

She laughed at the thought of having to relay that to anyone.

Services began at 8:00 Sunday mornings, according to the marquee, then again at 11:00. Wednesday's were reserved for Bible Study/Prayer Meeting, at 7:00 p.m.

The massive white structure sat on ten acres of manicured green lawn, dotted here and there with lush myrtle and ash trees.

The four squared building was identical on its four sides. Each entrance was flanked by three magnificent ten feet high white double doors.

Twelve doors total allowed access into the building, three on the East, three on the North, three on the South, and still, three on the West.

Four straight unadorned white columns arrayed across the aperture of each white stoned porch stood like giant guardian angels defying anyone or anything to defile the space between them.

The majestic columns supported a massive roof measuring 106,500 square feet, housing a grand steeple that soared dizzyingly; it appeared to the awe struck observer, to the highest heavens.

For the sake of going green, cylindrical solar panels lined each side of the flat roof, giving the much needed energy saving support. Well placed skylights saturated the sanctuary below with natural light from above.

"I wonder if this is where my sister and Donnie worship. I know Etta Mae, but not so much Donnie is always in somebody's church. This must be the one they belong to."

She stood there for quite some time, lost in thought. From her standpoint, the wide white paneled doors appeared to beckon her wayward soul to enter deep into its holistic walls.

"My, my, my, how majestic and pure you are in all your splendor!" She voiced aloud.

"It could be the most important decision you'll ever make in your lifetime."

The gawking New Yorker swung sharply around, startled beyond belief by the deep baritone voice.

A tall, broadly built black Adonis, the color of smooth, dark chocolate impeccably dressed, she guessed to be in his early fifties had exited a glistening white 2012 Lincoln Navigator.

The white tailored suit made of the finest silk appeared to all but shimmer in the bright sun light. Her eyes followed the long, lean legs down to the whitest of white Italian leather shoes.

Short hair brushed into a perfected 360 wave pattern, graying at the temples, framed a square-jawed face.

A well-trimmed salt and pepper mustache sat between a broad nose and full dark lips. Those same ample lips parted in the most welcoming smile, revealing perfect white teeth.

"Oh my, his parents must have paid a fortune for those pearly whites."

Dee thought it to be virtually impossible for the perfect choppers to belong to any human.

She suddenly found her small trembling hand become engulfed in a warm vacuum. But just as quickly, she withdrew it and absently wiped her hand on the front of her tailored shorts.

"This gentleman's presence makes me so uneasy."

Donnie had warned her to be careful. She stole another quick look at his face. "There's something unnerving about his eyes."

"Hello, young lady, I'm Master Prophet, Eli Cummings." He watched the nervous woman closely. "You're new around here, aren't you? I mean, I've never seen you in this neighborhood."

"Ah, uh, no, I mean yes...I mean n-no I'm not." Dee stammered.

"Yes, you're new or no you're from the neighborhood...which is it?"

"No, I'm not from here. I just flew in town on yesterday, in fact, from New York. I'm visiting my sister and her husband."

She looked past the tall figure to the street, and wondered how she could escape this creepy close encounter.

"Et-Etta Mae and Donnie LeRoy Smith. Etta Mae's my oldest sister."

"I know them. Your sister is a staunch warrior on the battlefield for the Lord. Now, as for Donnie, well....

For the most part, he does have a heart for God, but I'm afraid the golfing range has become his lord."

"Oh, so you're their pastor, I mean they are members here?"

"No, they are not members of this church, but what is good about it all, is that they do belong to God's *Church*."

"Oh, I just thought...

"And what about you?" He sternly asked. "What church are you affiliated with?"

"Oh no, here we go! Now he's gone and done it." She thought. "Why'd he have to go and ask that question?"

He patiently waited for the answer to his suspicions.

"W-ell...." She slowly responded. "How can I put this? When I was little, my grandmother took us to... In fact I, ah, that is, w-we were baptized there. I-I mean, my sisters and I were baptized at St. Stephen's Missionary Baptist Church, in Carterville, North Carolina."

"Oh, I see... and that wasn't so hard, now was it?" the Prophet asked.

"Your grandmother obviously did her part and that was to teach you about the Lord, but the rest; accepting Him into your heart was up to you."

He said this, fully knowing the woman's belief system was on shaky grounds from the start. He had only asked her the soul-searching question in order to put a voice to her stand on faith, or lack thereof.

Her agnostic view of God meant that somewhere deep down she had once believed, but had rationalized at some time or other, in her life that He didn't exist.

"Huh?" Dee fidgeted and looked down. The uneasiness she felt had become more pronounced by each passing moment.

153

"I-I guess y-you could say that."

"Now your sister Cynthia—

"H-How do you know about Cyndi? I didn't tell you I had a sister by that name!"

She began to backup; ready to bolt from the strange man's all-knowing presence.

"Why would a good and merciful God allow your parents to perish?" That's the question you two wanted answered."

"Well, if He's so good, why would He?"

"Delilah," the prophet began, "from the years you were with Mrs. Collins, your grandmother, I know you learned that the 'adversary' the devil was the only one who "comes to steal, to kill, and to destroy.

No one ever stops to blame the one responsible for the catastrophes in the world, but instead, prefers to blame God.

If it is written that, "Jesus came so that we may have life, and have it more abundantly. Then could you please tell me how death and destruction could come from those words."

The prophet watched her mull the words over in her head. He led the trembling woman to a nearby bench embossed with an advertisement.

"Only Heaven's water is purer. Come! Drink from the 'Well'; you'll never thirst again!" They sat down.

"There's a word of knowledge for you, Mrs. Delilah Carol Collins Melvin Cox Williams Simmons Jefferson Whitman, the prophet said without pausing to breathe.

"And it is… you're only bound by what you allow to bind you."

She rose to flee, but the astonished woman found it virtually impossible to pull away. She was more restrained by his knowledge of her life's history than by a physical grip.

"You sound exactly like my sister! Is there no end to my torment?"

"Yes," he said, "there is an end, but only you know how, and only you know when. The power is yours."

"The power is mine?" She asked through tears. "You mean I have the power to lose this heavy burden I've been carrying of my husband's betrayal!" You're saying I have the power of freeing myself of non-commitment? I have the power to—

"To forgive your husband of his infidelity, for the hurt, the shame, and the humiliation he's caused you? Yes! Delilah, the power lies within you. And He is called the Holy Spirit."

"What do you mean, the Holy Spirit?" she questioned defiantly, "I don't even believe there is a God let alone a spirit that's holy and supposedly living in me! And besides, you don't know what that man did to me!"

"You're wrong, I do know, and I also know where he is now."

"Now... right now... You're telling me you know where my trifling husband is... right at this very moment."

"Yes, my dear, I do."

"Oh; okay, so you got it like that; I'm impressed, but forgive me if I don't ask where he is, 'cause I don't care."

"Yes, you do care, but at the moment you're thinking with your emotions."

"Yes, I am angry and I'll never forgive that traitor."

"Even you must know that there's no sin too great or too small that is not covered under the blood of the Savior, Jesus Christ."

"W-well, forgiving someone is a pretty tall order in my book."

"No, you're wrong, but there is one sin that is un-forgivable and you, unfortunately, are treading dangerous waters."

"Oh, and just how, exactly, am I doing that, may I ask?" She stood up and so did he.

"Simply by your choice to hold on to the unsavory belief that God doesn't exist, or your wanting proof that He does. You were taught to know better."

"So tell me, where's all this love He's supposed to have for us?"

Ironically, the stranger already knew that the brave front the troubled woman displayed was nothing more than a safety net she'd erected to keep from falling.

"You have felt Him tugging at your heart-string, but you continue to be in a state of denial and saying no to his Holy Spirit. And *that*, my dear child, is called 'blasphemy,' the unpardonable sin."

"So, what exactly makes it unpardonable?"

"Think about it! When a person confesses his sins and asks Christ into his heart, that person is then saved. The Spirit of Christ comes to dwell within his spirit.

Fortunately, he no longer listens to his soul-man but instead listens to his spirit-man. That's how we'll able to choose between right and wrong."

He stared intensely into her eyes, as he continued to explain.

"The Holy Spirit is our conscience. However, if you never ask Him in, or believe on Him, then when you die, and since your sins haven't been pardoned; guess where you end up."

"Hell?"

"In Hell."

"Oh… since you know me so well," Dee contended. "I don't have to tell you that I also don't believe in Hell either.

Like I said before; since your God loves us so much then why would He send the ones He loves to torment?"

"Young lady, do you hear yourself? Do you hear what you are saying?"

"Yes! I know exactly what I'm saying, and I'm not the only one who's said it either! So there!"

"Well," the stranger went on to say, "what you just said proves to me that you do know deep down in your soul that the God you supposedly have rejected is a good God.

You know in your heart that God does not send anyone to torment, because He said in 3 John 2: "Beloved, concerning all things, I wish that you may prosper and be in good health, even as your soul prospers."

"Who *or* what exactly are you?" Dee asked, unable to refute the remark. "Are you an angel?"

"Who, or what do you think I am?"

"I don't have a clue, that's why I asked you." She backed away. Something she seemed to be doing a lot while she conversed with this stranger.

"Well, in that case, I can be who or whatever you want me to be at this particular moment." He offered. "I do know that right now you need me to be a listening and non-judgmental ear that can shed light in your darkness. To give answers to the burning questions that's tearing you up inside."

She sensed a quieting in her spirit and pondered the many questions lying dormant. The stranger remained quiet, patiently waiting for the onslaught to burst forth.

"Okay then, since you seem to have all the ready answers.... Pray tell me how this mind, body and spirit thing works. Are not they all the same?"

"May I take a seat, please?" The prophet sat down once again, not waiting for a response.

"Oh, is it going to be that long and drawn out?"

He simply looked at the inquisitive woman and patted the seat next to him. She hesitantly sat down, but left considerable space between them.

"You see, my dear, man is made up of three components." He began. "Spirit, soul and body—

"Duhh!" Dee interjected. "You don't have to be an Einstein to know that!"

"Allow me to finish, please." The stranger said. If I'm not mistaken, I believe I've already covered that."

"Oops... Sorry, I wasn't listening." Dee apologized.

"Apology accepted. Now then, when you're a believer, God then dwells in your spirit and communicates with your regenerated spirit, which then saturates your soul, allowing man to become transformed to express Him. Romans 12: 2b "Be ye transformed by the renewing of your mind.""

"Wow! So, let me see if I got this straight." Dee finally said. "If I understand you correctly, you're actually saying....

When or if my body is occupied and directed by the Spirit of God, then His Spirit talks to me through my spirit, and uses my body for His purpose."

"That's right...You get life with a purpose."

"Wow! That's some deep shi—

"Uh mm! Now, the reason I said you are in danger of blaspheming, is because you've personally chosen to disconnect your phone line so to speak.

"My phone line, you say?"

"Yes, your phone line, and that, however, could very well be your answer to finding inner peace."

"Like understanding why I find myself marrying and marrying again." She naively stated.

The man said nothing, but instead opted to allow the perplexed woman to draw her own conclusions. It seemed like an eternity before she spoke again.

"Speaking of marriage, how can God help me with the situation I'm finding myself in now?"

She posed the question to herself more so than to the stranger. Again, her pondering questions were met with total silence.

"Oh, I see, now you're giving me the old silent treatment."

"Some of life's many questions are only meant to be answered by the one who's asking them. He finally said.

"Albeit, I can tell you this... do you remember the slogan made popular some few years ago?"

"What slogan are you referring to?"

"WWJD! What would Jesus do? Remember?"

"Hummm.... What would Jesus do indeed? Hmmm." She carefully thought before answering.

The stranger patiently waited for her answer.

"Let's see... I think He would forgive; yes that's exactly what He'd do. He would simply for-give. Now isn't that just like Him?"

"And there you have it!"

The prophet proclaimed, smiling warmly. That which he'd finally heard from a woman who'd lost her way was music to his ears.

The now enlightened woman was about to re-dig the wells of her salvation that her beloved grandmother once helped her to dig. But his jubilation was short lived.

"*Hel-lo!* In case you haven't noticed, I'm not Him, I'm not Jesus!" Dee's statement had dispelled his assumptions. "That's way too tall of an order!"

"Not if you would just allow His Spirit to communicate with your spirit, it isn't."

Her statement had bought the prophet back to the task at hand. He went on to further explain.

"It can only be done by asking for the Spirit of Forgiveness."

"Oh damn… I mean, darn!"

Unbridled tears welled up and ran down the woman's face and fell on the expensive silk blouse.

"Now look what I've done! This is virgin silk!" She attempted to explain. "Water and real silk don't mix, you know."

"Yes, I know, but you my dear have much to think about and much soul searching to do.

"I do?"

"Yes, you do… And I'm afraid I'll have to leave you to do just that."

He started to rise from the bench. "I pray you peace and I pray you understanding."

"Wait! Don't go!"

She instinctively reached out to block his rising. A frantic moment was frozen in time. Finally, the prophet resettled onto the bench.

Thoughts of despair ran through his mind. He had hoped that just maybe, a break-through to the torn-soul seated beside him had occurred.

"Its…it's just that I don't know what to do about my husband."

"What about him; him and mankind in general for that matter?"

'I'm… I'm just lost as to what decision to make is all.'

Her head was bowed so low, the next question came out in a whisper.

"What made him do this to me?" Sobbing, she lifted her bowed head and cried out. "Jesus! Help Me!"

The 'Man of God' offered her his white handkerchief. He shifted uneasily in his seat before attempting to give any semblance of an explanation. It pleased him, however, to hear the unbeliever call on a name she probably had not called on since childhood. Yet… there was always hope.

"Romans One." He began. "Around verse twenty-five or so; 'Man, God's creation, through 'the Fall' had become vain and took on the attributes of Satan.

Though man knew God, he did not thank Him or glorify Him. And in doing so, the Creator gave man up to the lusts of his heart so that he could dishonor his own body."

"W-*what*?" The increased wrinkles and frown on the woman's forehead alerted the prophet that he needed to break the wording down to her level of understanding.

"I said all that to say this;man fell in love with himself, therefore, he chose to love what looked like himself over the One who had created him."

"You mean—

"Wait!" He said. "I mean that man was given over to uncleanness, passions of dishonor and a disapproved mind, because through the fault of the enemy; man didn't really see God for who He is.

The Creator is not the author of confusion, but you can't say that about the 'enemy.'The enemy's mind will have a man thinking he's a woman, and a woman thinking that she's a man. In their mind, they think they can only love what looks like them. Scripture tells us, "Let the mind be in you that was also in Christ Jesus."

So, if you don't have His mind, then it's easier for the mind of the enemy to be supplanted in one's thoughts."

"Whew… it's all too complicated for me." Dee stated.

"Well maybe this will help you. To think in the flesh or to be carnal minded, a man can lie with a man, and a woman can lie with a woman with no qualms."

Dee finally understood, but thought it to be a bit too far fetched.

"That's exactly what I'm saying." He stated. "Look around you, is not man the only creation who can choose to go against what he was designed for?"

"Hey, now that you've put it that way… Man is the only hardheaded creation there is!" Satan realizes that and only comes after man and not animals, per se, to do the opposite of what God designed him to do."

She slapped her hands together with excitement and shouted.

"Hot damn! Oo, sorry."

"Simply because Man was made in the image of God, and if he's the enemy of God, then guess what he is to us!"

"That old piece of crap!" Dee shouted.

"Now, I must say, in all fairness… to be truthfully honest, sin is sin and no one sin is greater than another. Fornication, adultery, murder, incest and slander are no less sin in the eyes of God than homosexuality, although he did call that certain act, an abomination.

"But to let man tell it, homosexuality is not sinful!" Dee snickered.

"The devil *is* a lie; and the father of lies." Prophet Cummings shook his head in disbelief.

"And people wonder why the Word says; "My people perish from the lack of knowledge. And oh, by the way, that scripture spoke of the lack of 'spiritual knowledge' that is."

"Maybe that's how judges are passing laws to legalize everything under the sun." Dee added.

"Hmmm…well, since you said that, then I can only quote 2 Chronicles 19: 6 on that one; "Consider carefully what you do, because you are not judging for man but for the Lord, who is with you whenever you give a verdict." In other words,"judge carefully" is the warning to the moral decision makers.

They had been talking for well over an hour. Fatigue weighed heavily on them both. They both thought heavily on the argumentative topics that had been discussed.

Just by knowing what was needed to make things right between her and God, caused Dee's head to sink low. She just could not bring herself to utter the fateful words of "Father, forgive me, for I have sinned."

Prophet Cummings watched the expression of indecision play across the woman's countenance. He knew she was on the verge of denouncing the benighted views she had once held, and were now ready to drink from the 'Well.' He would not be surprised at the remark he would hear come from the now enlightened disciple.

A sense of calmness settled over her anxious spirit. There was just something about this man of God. But… she couldn't exactly put her finger on it.

"You know… I feel like the "woman at the well." She finally said to the stranger. "You have surely given me 'living water' to drink. Now out of my belly shall surely flow oceans, not rivers, but oceans of this living water! I must go now!" She rose to leave.

"I must run, and I must *tell* everyone how sweet the 'water' is from this '*Well*!' From which I just drank."

And she did just that, leaving her long ago discarded shoes behind, as she did so. For some reason, she had been unable to keep them on her feet. The luscious green grass had felt like velvet under her feet, soothing and comforting. After she had ran a few feet away, the now liberated woman looked down and realized that she was shoeless.

Another cloudy haze had miraculously descended when she turned back. It was so thick Dee could barely make out the tall figure that stood in the space she'd just vacated.

She also remembered that she hadn't thanked the Master Prophet for the Water he had verbally poured into her life and ran back through the mist.

The 'Stranger' welcomed her with open arms and the two embraced. She felt so protected in his arms and thought how she could've stayed there forever.

Finally, the embrace was broken, and they both stepped away. No words were spoken as she looked deep into his eyes for the very first time. Her eyes widened as she seemingly drowned in the 'pools of love' that to her were deeper than the deepest sea.

"My Child." He simply said and took a hold of Dee's hand. She fell to her knees.

Extreme emotions over shadowed the kneeling woman. The repenting woman sobbed uncontrollably while she held tightly to his comforting hands. She let go of one hand long enough to wipe the tears from her eyes.

She no longer saw the brilliant white leather shoes as she looked down, but instead, she saw bare, nail scarred-feet. She raised her head and quickly inspected his wrists.

To her astonishment, there were nail prints.

Suddenly everything came into focus, leaving the former agnostic to cry out.

"My Lord and My God! Forgive me and come into my life!"

Those same nail scarred hands lifted the forlorn woman to her feet.

"Delilah Collins, you were forgiven a long time ago." He said."My peace I give you and my peace I leave you."

"I-I was, even after I denied you?"

"There was once a friend of mine who denied me three times ... and I forgave him three times."

"So, what you're saying is ... you never tire of forgiving us."

"Yes, that is true."

"No, that is love."

He smiled the warmest smile ever, before he said to her.

"Go now, daughter and do what is right in your heart."

Dee covered her face with her hands as uncontrollable sobs racked her delivered soul. She couldn't ever recall shedding so many tears, but this time these were soothing tears of joy. When next she looked up, it was apparent she was alone. Even the magnificent, white edifice had disappeared.

Ironically, it didn't matter to her. She did not feel alone, because somewhere in the recesses of her spirit she heard the words; "I'll never leave you, nor forsake you." The woman now knew the Stranger was no longer a stranger. He was her God!

Suddenly the world seemed brighter; her soul felt lighter. Birds chirped, and vibrant colored butterflies flickered about. With her head thrown back in total abandonment, Dee found herself spinning around and around.

The blue sky was filled with enormous white cumulus clouds. She stopped abruptly. It suddenly registered that she still hadn't thanked the Man of God. So, she uttered those very words, andcried out with a loud voice.

"Thank you! Thank you Jesus!"

From out of nowhere she heard an audible voice say;

"No, daughter; thank you for letting me bless you. Welcome home."

"I may never know just how long I would have gone before stopping to realize that my 'Redeemer' lives." Dee thought to herself.

She became so over whelmed with the sense of gratitude that an unrehearsed shout of *"Hallelujah,"* exploded from her lips.

"Thank you! Thank you! Thank you! Dee shouted from the top of her voice. Then she picked up her shoes and danced down the street with the tune, "I Can See Clearly Now' the rain is gone, actively playing in her head.

CHAPTER

"Are you finally ready to tell me about what's really going on with you?" Etta Mae asked Tonika. "You and Stephanie had a secret code going on back there for a minute. And don't think I didn't notice!"

"Why, what-ev-a' do you mean, Miss Et-ta?" Tonika said in her best southern drawl. "I don't have a clue what you're talking 'bout."

Tonika felt as if there were a lot she didn't know. "This is so unusual, I share everything with Etta Mae," she thought to herself, "but this time it's different. For one thing I haven't even come to grips with this bombshell myself."

"When you're ready, my friend, you will tell me, but only when you're ready." She gave the trembling hand a gentle squeeze. "And I'll be here when you are."

Etta Mae could sense the turmoil her friend was going through. From what little was shared this morning, she knew it definitely had something to do with Josh.

"You truly are a dear friend. Thanks for understanding." Etta Mae gave Tonika's shoulder a reassuring rub.

"Hmmm, that's funny, look at that, I never noticed that store before." Tonika' eyes followed her friend's gaze to 'Surreptitious,' a shop seductively staged with women's intimate apparel.

Tonika moved over to the window for a closer inspection. A'barely there' pink see-through garment seductively arrayed on a mulatto toned mannequin dominated the window display.

Shades of red dominated the interior of the boutique. Red delicate lace bras in the form of strapless, mini-misers, convertibles and wonder-wires, were amply displayed throughout the show room. "A sure natural fit for any body size," read the caption for the delicate apparels.

Revealing panties, bustiers in animal prints and solids lay folded on rounded red organza covered tables. Etta Mae took a seat on a nearby bench, and picked up a discarded brochure.

She began to casually thumb through it. The featured cover was emblazoned with intimate articles of clothing. ***"Only she knows where her power is hidden."*** *T*he sassy slogan read.

"Lingerie' meant to be worn under any formative business suit, or elegant gown, giving the wearer the feeling of power to take charge, and most importantly feel seductive."

'***Surreptitious,***' meaning 'hidden things' were boldly printed on the vibrant red and black pamphlet cover. It was a brochure from the intimate apparel boutique before them. The brochure featured the same articles of clothing displayed in the window.

The boutique it seemed was founded by a Jessie Devlin, of Lower Crescent, New York, in collaboration with his wife, Wicca. The Devlin's design of intimate apparel was highly prized among their risqué clientele.

Fantasy designs made up a large portion of the Devlin line, accommodating the most daring at heart. French maidens, red-hot she devils, leopard skins, bunnies, you name it. Alluring bras and panties crafted only for the bold and the beautiful were the mainstay of the collection.

The *'Jazzy Jezzie'* Line, a cohesive collection of red seductive, alluring, matte nylon and Chantilly lace bras, thongs, boy shorts and beyond were the most popular items sold. Each piece was delicately constructed to mix or match. This line of intimate wear embodied the very essence of its namesake, *'Jezebel.'*

Etta Mae was flabbergasted by a warning written in small print. **Caution: A sudden feeling of domination may overtake the unbridled wearer of this garment. Be careful to never expose the undergarments to sunlight when worn.**

"Ooo-wee! Those '*JazzieJezzies*' are some dangerous undies!"

Etta Mae shared the pamphlet with Tonika.

"Look at this... they almost come to life it looks like, if the light catches them while you're wearing them."

"My, my, that's stupid!"

Tonika took the pamphlet. Her mouth dropped in disbelief.

"I tell you what Etta Mae; anytime any 'drawers' of mine come to life by themselves, you better shoot me dead!" The look of shock on her friend's face led her to add. "For real though, I ain't lying."

"Okay, I can do that for you, but just remember, you asked." Laughter was shared, and then Etta Mae paused for a moment. "Those 'JazzieJezzies' are something fierce, not unlike their namesake, I might add." She chuckled to herself before commenting on the antics of the biblical character.

As the two ladies are talking, a miraculous transformation was taking place nearest the store's front entrance. A store mannequin had begun to transpose.

"Tonika, now you do know that Eve wasn't the only woman in the Bible who had her man under thumb, don't you?"

"You mean there's more?"

"Yes, Mam, you bet there was more. There was that Jezebel!"

"Jezebel, I've heard about her, just last week..."

"Umph! Now that girl was b-b-bad to the bone!"

Do you think it's safe to bring... you know, her name up?" Tonika did a quick glance around. "I mean, you know what happened earlier."

"Now, my girl Jezzie was queen of all the vixens. She got things done without her man even knowing how it was done. Lies, were how she did it, you know. My girl was a straight faced 'liar!'"

"What makes you say that?" "Because, honey... Jezebel was so evil, even Jesus talked about her in Revelation 2."

"Well, she must've been bad then, if Jesus talked about her. She probably ranked right up there with the Pharisees, and the Sadducees."

"Look at you! Go on with you bad self!" Etta Mae exclaimed.

"You see, I do have retaining power."

"Yes, I see… but back to the scarlet lady; now it's said if you're not careful her spirit will take over your body, even today. And it doesn't matter if you're a man, or a woman."

"Oh, so that explains why it says if you wear her namesake, you're bound to become a dominatrix of sorts." Tonika reasoned. "Ummm, maybe, that's the answer to my problem. Note to self; buy 'Jezzie' wear!"

"Oh, I wouldn't do that if I were you." Etta Mae warned. "Why would you want to look like a 'floozy' anyway? You know Black women are already stereotyped as Jezebels!"

"Are you serious? Etta, I swear you're a walking, talking encyclopedia." Tonika chided. "I didn't know that. And where'd you get it from anyways?"

"You may don't know it, but I do read other books besides the Bible."

"I know you're well read, so lay it on me, sistah. What's my lesson today?"

"Well, for your moment in Black History, I'm quoting something I gleaned from a paper written by a Dr. David Pilgrim at the Ferris State University's Jim Crow Museum.

He called it the Jezebel Stereotype. According to the paper, Jezebel was depicted as a "Black woman with an insatiable appetite. Stereotyping black women as Jezebels were used during slavery as a rationalization for sexual relations between slavers, and their slaves."

Apparently, that's the reason we were raped by 'Massa', whenever and wherever. You get me?"

"Whew! How can that be?" Tonika inquired. "You mean to say Jezebel was powerful, and horny, too? Now that's a destructive combination!"

Tonika thought of the conversation she'd had with Edna Brown two weeks ago.

Edna had given her a printout on the wiles of the horrible woman. She hadn't taken the time to read it but had stuffed it in her purse, hoping to look it over later.

"Tonika, you are too much!"

"Okay, here is what else it said. "Black women were thought of in Jim Crow's days as being lascivious by nature."

"The adjectives that were used to categorize us were: seductive, alluring, worldly, beguiling, tempting and lewd.

Now get this, White women were thought of as self-respectful, self-controlled, and modest."

"But I thought you were only called that if you were light skinned, you know, mullatto, with long hair, and a coke bottle shape. And oh, don't forget voluptuous red lips!" Tonika's pouted lips made both women chuckle.

They are so engrossed in their conversation, that neither noticed the eerie figure that moved towards them.

"True 'dat, true 'dat," Etta Mae laughingly commented, "but to 'Massa', any female form, no matter what she looked like, was just a dark crevice to sink his flag pole in."

"Ummph, and my poor foremothers were called every name in the book. Now, I learned they were even called Jezebels." Tonika commented.

"Shucks girl, who knows, maybe 'Massa' put bags over their heads."

"Let's just say, over our less attractive foremothers' heads. Oh and to be fair, that paper also stated that your foremothers were even raped by your own forefathers. And since it was the norm, the poor things didn't have a defense."

"Umph, umph, umph," Tonikagrunted, and solemnly shook her head. "My people, my people!"

Dark blank eyes with eyelids painted every hue of the rainbow stared pointedly at the two unsuspecting women.

A chained gold nose ring reached from the left ear to a nostril adorned a smooth flawless face. The headdress and jewelry told of her regal position. The small frame, average figure of a woman was covered from head to toe, as the tradition of a Phoenician princess warranted.

Thin pale arms that once hung lifeless ended in long tapered manicured fingers, painted the most brilliant red.

The ladies were startled when the airways became filled with the pulsating beat of '*Bad Girls.*' The loud music had over taken the soothing piano concerto.

Gold ornaments worn on the formidable phantom figure's ankles jingled distractedly as she stealthily made her way toward the befuddled women.

"Uh oh, let the games begin!" Tonika watched terrified and yelled over the pounding beat. "I bet cha' anything that's old Jezzie!"

"Well, if it isn't the 'Painted Lady' herself… in the flesh!" Etta Mae yelled back, with both fingers in her ears.

The music died down as Jezebel began to speak. She paced to and fro in front of the women.

"*I know, I know, you two ladies probably think of me as the hussy of all hussies! Now, don't you?*" She blazed at the startled women. "*But honey, if you had a man like mine, you would do what I did.*"

"Well, if you want to go there, you won't get any argument from me."

Tonika returned the stare and thought of something the angels always said in the Bible when they visited a human.

"I have a question for you. How come you spirits don't ever say, "Fear not," like the angels do? You just show up, and start talking as if someone's been expecting you."

"*Mrs. Gibbons, I presume?* Jezebel asked. "*My name alone, strikes fear in people's hearts as it is, so why would I waste words on something so trivial?*" Smiling wickedly, she shouted. "*Boo!*" Then she went on to ask. "*So, are you scared or not?*"

Tonika's hands flew to her mouth, stifling a gasp.

"Is my name popular with you spirits today or something?"

"*Yes, I have to say, it has been discussed a time or two.*" Jezebel retorted flippantly.

"By whom?"

"*It doesn't matter; I just came to set the record straight! You two were talking about me just then. I fail to see the reason why I'm on everyone's mind and lips. I'm not as bad as everyone make me out to be.*"

"Come again! Woman, I know you don't even believe that, yourself." Etta Mae said.

"Well, at least I was good to my husband, who was a big wuss. There once was something he wanted and he couldn't have, he pouted and wouldn't eat for days! And do you know why?"

"No, why?"

"Naboth, our neighbor, the Jezreelite wouldn't sell him, and by him, I mean King Ahab, his land. That's why!" Jezebel lamented. *"That land had been in this man's family for years. "Now you know he wasn't about to give his land up don't you? Would you?"*

"I know I wouldn't, and if anyone tried to take it, they would have a hell of a fight on their hands!" Tonika declared.

"And guess why he wanted the land? Go on guess!"

"I don't know…maybe to add to his possessions, maybe…" Etta Mae said.

"You're the one telling the story, so tell us why he wanted it." Tonika said.

"Oh, I see you are the smart aleck…. Okay, here it is. Ahab that was his name you know…"

"Yes, you told us. It's not like I—Tonika started to say.

"He wanted the land to extend that little garden of his!"

Jezebel yelled louder than she had intended.

"His garden, what's a king doing with a garden?" Tonika asked.

"And you're asking me? All I know is that he had one! Okay!"

The conversation went back and forth between Jezebel and Tonika. Etta Mae merely watched as each woman battled to outdo the other. Jezebel went on to further explain the situation that'd surrounded her husband's garden.

"I mean really, Tonika!" Jezebel threw both hands up in annoyance.

Tonika squirmed uneasily. She'd somehow gotten use to the unexpected presence of apparitions, but to be personally identified by them was something different.

"It was getting old I tell you, all that whining. So I said to the king, let's be real, is this the way a king supposed to act? Get up and eat, and cheer up! Ole Jez' got your back!"

"Yea, and I heard, or read rather, how you handled your business, girl!" Etta Mae chimed in.

"I was on it! As you say nowadays. You know it! Shucks half of the time my husband didn't even know how I did business! But, you know we women do have our ways."

"I don't know Jezzie, I don't think anyone could be as conniving, and as manipulative as you, girlfriend. Like I told Tonika, you're queen of them all. I'd say you got us all beat."

"Well thanks for the compliment!"

Jezzie's high pitch laugher nearly pierced the ladies ear drums; they covered their ears.

"To pick up where I left off..."

But before she could continue Etta Mae wanted to know about her dealings with Elijah, the Prophet.

"Wait, wait, wait, what I'd like to know is, why did you threaten my man Elijah?"

"Elijah! You talking to me about that—Jezebel shouted.

"Now why'd you bring that pest up?"

"I don't know, I just wondered why you pursued him like a hound dog."

"That man killed all my prophets! And when he messed with my livelihood, then he had to go! He'd just better be glad I didn't catch his pesky ..."

"Yes, I know, but you did—

"Enough about that prophet already! Here's how it went down with Ahab.

For starters, I forged Ahab's name on a letter accusing Naboth of a crime, which he never committed. I sealed it, sent it to the officials, and had two rascals speak against him in court."

"O! You were a sneaky something. And a controlling one at that!" Declared Tonika.

"Hee, hee, I know! Sometimes I even surprise myself!" Then in a more somber tone she added.

"If that's what you want to call it. It got the job done didn't it?"

"Oooh! She told you girlfriend. I tell you what, let's let her finish. I want to hear more."

"Thank you, Mam." Jezebel made a mock bow to Etta Mae.

"Well needless to say, the man was found guilty, and was stoned to death."

"O! Ouch!" Tonika proclaimed. "What a shame, that poor man."

"So, King Ahab got that land he wanted."

"Yes, but at what price?" Etta Maeasked. "The poor man was minding his own business, and look what happened, it was so sad."

"Poor nothing, you do whatever it takes, I always say! And besides, I just loved asserting my power!"

Jezebel dismissed Etta Mae's display of sympathy with a wave of her hand.

"I just bet you did."

Etta Mae always prided herself on being a fair judge of character, but out of all the villains in the Bible, this one topped the cake. She found herself disliking the conniving, manipulative, control freak of a female specimen, tremendously.

The women's dislike of her had no bearings on Jezebel; she hadn't gotten to be the most powerful woman in her day by caring what anyone thought. She'd possessed power, and that was all that mattered. She made it a point to never sweat the small stuff.

"It is said you know, behind every great man, stands an even greater woman!" Now am I right?"

"No, honey, I wouldn't say you were great; I would say you were more like trifling!" Tonika said. "And for the record, we don't stand behind our men, we stand beside them!"

"You tell her, Toni!" Etta Mae shouted proudly. But neither woman expected the venom that spewed forth.

"Oh, and you're standing with yours, Tonika?"

A calculating laugh followed as Jezebel knowingly looked Tonika squarely in the eye.

"Ain't no use of going home... Joshie's packed his bags and gone." The wicked harpy sang.

"I am so sick of this!" Tonika exclaimed.

She tearfully threw her hands up in surrender.

"I'm sick of everybody, or everything knowing my damn business!"

"Well now that you know..."

May I finish without anymore interruptions, please?"

"Tonika, girl you're not making any friends here."

Etta Mae pulled her friend down within ear shot and whispered.

"So I would be careful if I were you; there's no telling what this thing may exact on us. So just be cool. Okay?"

"By all means, continue Jezebel, and Tonika don't interrupt her again. Okay?"

"Oh, alright, but you have to admit—

Etta Mae's look of disapproval cut the remark short.

Jezebel was satisfied with the reaction she'd gotten and proceeded with her tale. The annoying human was finally silenced.

"Now, where was I?" The ghost figure began. *"So, things were going just super, until that pesky prophet Elijah came on the scene! But I even had him going too.*

"Oh, so now she wants to talk Elijah!"

The sidekick wanted so badly to speak but was fortunately able to restrain herself.

"But alas, even I had to pay to the piper. I had to heed the voice of God, and my fate wasn't a pretty one. *I'm sure all of you've heard the story how I was thrown from a window by two ungrateful servants of mine.*

It just goes to show, you just-can't-get- good help... Those old 'balless bastards' listened to that rascal Jehu instead of listening to me!"

Tonika jumping to her feet was unable to contain her emotions any further let out a big cheer.

"Yeaaah! Go Jehu!" Then she said to Jezebel."It served you right. You finally got your come-uppance!"

"I'm glad my untimely demise made your day!"

"Can you blame us?"

"No, I don't put anything past you two, but to top it all off, this man Jehu... well his chariot runs over me after I was thrown over the balcony. Then those mangy dogs devoured my body! The only things left were my head and feet!"

"Eeewww! Gross!" Etta Mae and Tonika both said together.

"Well, it wasn't like you weren't warned. You received a prophecy "the dogs were going to lick your blood." Etta Mae commented.

"So I did, so I did, but all this beautiful body, gone! You had to know it wasn't a pretty site."

"I'm sure it wasn't;I can't even imagine." Etta Mae said.

"Thanks for your sympathy."

"You're welcome, any time."

"If only I could turn back the hands of time! Why... why I would be a different woman!"

Jezebel lamented as she walked away from the two awe struck women. She returned to her position in the boutique, and transitioning once again into a lifeless mannequin.

The ladies sat for a while, and continued to stare in the store front.

"So the old bad girl got her due. Imagine being eaten by dogs, umph! They say the old girl's spirit still lives on, and we saw it for ourselves today! So it is definitely true!"

"Ya' think! Now don't you go buying any of her underwear, because I wouldn't be able to handle another of her kind."

"Who're you telling? None of that Chantilly lace is touching any of this!"

"And who have you been talking to that you know about her spirit?"

"What do you mean?"

"You sounded as if you knew something about her before I told you."

"Oh, I ran into Sister Edna Brown a few days ago."

"Motor-mouth Edna? Come on let's get out of here, I'm kind of drained. Aren't you?"

The two ladies picked up their purses and started for the exit.

"Edna's always humming, *Blessed Assurance, Jesus in Mine* every Sunday! I found myself humming it this morning."

"She has a way of getting to you. She always sits in the third row on the left side of the church, and her mouth is always going."

The women walk faster than usual. They weren't interested in having another encounter. Three were enough for the day.

"God bless her; if you ask how she's doing, have some time on your hand, because for an hour or so you'll have to hear her testimony."

"What's her favorite line ... "Lord, I'm blessed and highly favored."

Hysterical laughter carried the two into the welcomed sunlight. They were elated to finally escape the dark and unearthly atmosphere inside the mall.

"Miss Edna broke it down to me child, she even gave me a page from let's see; um, um, hum, hum, hum. Oh! Here it is... something she got off the web about 'Jezebel in Our Society' by this Albatrus man."

Tonika pulled the piece of paper from her purse and began to read the contents.

"Listen to what it says."

"The Jezebel spirit is born of witchcraft and rebellion. This demon is one of the most common spirits in operation today, both in the church and in the world, and it is a powerful enemy of the body of Christ. She operates freely on sincere believers whose hearts are for God individually, and has also attained positions of power as powers and principalities within the Church. This spirit establishes its stronghold primarily in women; however, many men have been victimized by it as well, where it functions as a "controlling" spirit.

The spirit of Jezebel is behind the daughter of Democracy, i.e. Feminism. The Spirit of Jezebel is basically a controlling spirit working through the lust of the flesh, and the lust of the eyes, and the pride of life. It has, in general, two aims:

To gain identity, glory, recognition, power, and satisfy the need for the "praises of men". This is a consequence of the desire for love and self-worth focused on SELF.

"Now that's deep." Etta Mae said.

Tonika continued reading, but paused long enough to agree.

"Now, ain't it though?"

Jezebel was and is a political figure and uses spiritual control and manipulation to exert influence.

"Ummph, I'm sure glad Edna enlightened you, now you have something to top what she knows!"

"You're right about that, but who'd believe it? Wait, there's more."

Once under this delusionary spirit, she takes them captive, disguises herself as the spirit of God, and allows false prophecy, idolatry and worldly practices to flourish."

"I'll stop right there, because after reading this, girlfriend... with what we just encountered. I'd say we were too up close, too personal for my taste."

"I know that's right, now I'm with you there." Etta Mae agreed. "I can't get away from here fast enough!"

Tonika folded the slip of paper and slid it back inside her purse.

"I think we should be glad we got out of there with our heads!"

The women moved on with a sense of urgency. The stifling heat inside the car soon dissipated with welcoming coolness.

Etta Mae backed the car out of the parking stall and aiming it towards the busy freeway.

The day's paranormal activity bounced around in their heads. A ringing cell phone broke the silence, which brought about a frantic search.

"That's mine." Etta Mae said. She maneuvered the car with one hand.

"Hello? *Cyndi!* How're you doing, honey?...That's good... I-I'm doing okay, now that I'm where it's cool...Uh, huh, uh, huh. Uh-huh, uh-huh.

"This is Cyndi."

Etta Mae listened while mouthing to her passenger.

"Girl, I haven't heard from you since...how was Hawaii? Great! Janet and Geoffrey said they enjoyed you... Yes, they called last Sunday— Donnie told you I was out shopping? Uh-huh. "*Ha, ha, ha,* I bet he did... Well actually we're on our way home and should be there in about ten to fifteen minutes.... No, Dee's not with me...Well, when I left she was taking a nap. Did Donnie say she wasn't there? Humph, then I couldn't tell you where she is. But let me ask you this...Do you know what's going on with her? Uh huh... No, she hasn't told me enough to know what's really going on. She begins to and then stops like it's too much to even talk about. Then she'll get into her Delilah Collins mode. *Ha, ha, ha.* Yes, you know our sister. Yes... that's right. But I do know it's got something to do with her husband though. Oh, you did? Ooh, girl that's something."

Etta Mae stole a look at her passenger, and shrugged her shoulders. She had a surprised look on her face.

"W-well, I tell you what, I'll call you back when I get home. I had an experience last night too. Did He show you anything else? Oh, okay, I see. Okay, sweetie, yeah, uh-huh, uh huh, I'll talk to you later. Love you too! Smooches! Bye now—Okay, I'll tell her baby, bye bye now."

"Cynthia even knows there's something going on with our sister."

"How? What does she know?"

"She said that she'd had a vision of our sister boarding a plane to come to me."

"Oh! Is Cynthia a psychic or something?"

"Well, she is deeply rooted; studying theology and such, so I don't doubt that she hasn't been given a spiritual gift or two. God does reward those who diligently seek Him you know."

"That could explain it, she could have the gift of knowledge."

"Yep, she could at that."

"After everything we've been through today, nothing surprises me."

Etta Mae raised her hand to heaven and prayed.

"Lord! Whatever you are doing right now… don't do it without me! *Please*, don't do it without me! Amen and amen!"

"Oh, oh, and Lord, don't forget about me, please!"

The two women fell silent once again. The drone of the car's tires reverberated in a rhythmic sound.

"I tested HIV positive!"

The dreaded words exploded out of Tonika's mouth like the Mount St. Helen's eruption.

She felt surprisingly relieved. The pent up stress was finally resolved. The secret that had sat in the pit of her stomach like a ton of bricks was finally out.

However, she was not prepared for the flood of hot blinding tears that cascaded down her face. The liberated woman sobbed uncontrollably, gulping air in between trembles.

"Honey! Are you alright?" Etta Mae asked genuinely concerned.

She pulled the car over into a vacant parking lot, suddenly needing to console her dear friend. Etta Mae put the car into park, allowing the engine to run the air conditioner for their comfort.

"Oh Toni, I'm so sorry, I never knew."

"I-I." The words she wanted to utter couldn't find their way past the knot in her throat, crying even more. "Don't talk, just let me hold you."

Etta Mae gathered her stricken friend in her arms, offering what comfort she was able to give.

"How had this happened?" She wondered.

Never in her wildest dreams could she ever imagine someone so close to her find themselves in such a situation.

The comforting companion soon realized the amount of fortitude her friend possessed to silently bare a burden of such magnitude. She would never, ever under estimate her again.

Not once had she ever let on that her very existence was in jeopardy. Perhaps sharing the Gospel with her through the years had solidified her faith for sure.

"So, where to from here, girlie?" Etta Mae somberly asked. "You have to find Josh and tell him, you know."

"Yes, I know." Tonika quietly said, without lifting her head. "Who knew just one little letter from a doctor could destroy your whole world."

She hadn't had any symptoms. According to the letter, she may've had it for some time, but weren't aware of it.

Clinical latent infection typically lasts 8 to 10 years. The letter had read. A few people stay in this stage even longer, but others progress to a more-severe disease much sooner.

After she read that statement Tonika somehow knew her husband's extra marital affair couldn't possibly be the culprit. Unless, it hadn't been his first.

In any case, she reasoned that she had been true to her marriage vows. The decision to text Josh, asking him to meet her at home was the next step.

"Who're you calling or texting rather?"

"I'm texting Josh to see if he would meet me at home. We didn't do much talking before, but maybe we can come to some resolution today."

Tonika looked at her best friend and solemnly asked. "Pray for me Etta Mae, please."

"Girl! You know I got you!"

Etta Mae reached over to take hold of her friend's hand.

"When do you go back to the doctor?"

"On Monday, I have an appointment for 10:00." Tonika sent the text to Josh. "There! It's done, now let's see what happens."

"Did you ask him any questions when you talked with him?" Etta Mae wanted to know. "And by the way, when did you find out, and why haven't you told me before now?"

"Slow your roll!" Tonika managed to say with a smile. "And no, we didn't talk… we just yelled at each other. I've just been so upset with finding that damn note—

"Tonika! How could something like that slip your mind? Do you know this ain't anything to play with?"

"Damn it, Etta Mae! Who goes to have your iron level checked and expect to hear you're HIV positive? And besides I haven't even come to grips with it myself."

"Wait a minute! You had a transfusion some years ago didn't you?"

"Yes, when Adrika—

"That's it! Tonika! That could be it!" Etta Mae said excitedly.

"I doubt it … And as far as that goes, it's not exactly like the opportunity has presented itself. You're either busy with Donnie, your sister, and not to mention with all those visitations today!"

"What about the drive to the mall? You could've told me then."

"Well, to be truthful friend, with something such as this, you don't know who to tell. Deep down, I knew you would be there for me and all, but sometimes even your friends turn on you out of fear. I'm sorry I didn't trust you to be there for me."

Etta Mae was truly concerned with her friend's well-being and was kind of pained she hadn't shared it with her.

It now made sense why their afternoon excursion was anything but jovial. But, in any case, she knew it would certainly benefit Tonika to look into the matter of the transfusion.

Tonika continued to talk but her cohort's mind was too deep in thought to hear what she said.

"I know we share a lot… but this is something that I wanted to discuss with my—she stopped short of saying my husband, but her mouth was unable to form the words.

She didn't even know if there would be a marriage after last night. This was unfortunate, because she really did believe in the sanctity of it. But, it takes two to make it work.

"I-I just wanted to discuss it with Josh first." She finally said. "And I know it's going to be hard, but there is light at the end of the tunnel. I just have to keep going."

"W-what? I'm sorry Toni…. What were you saying? My mind—

"I was saying—never mind." Tonika interjected. "I'll discuss everything with you later."

Silence enveloped the car once again. As they neared home, rampant thoughts flickered through each of their minds.

CHAPTER
Seventeen

....

"Now there you go again…" Damian said, now feeling a bit uneasy while conspicuously inspecting every darkened corner of the spacious living room.

"Okay, suit yourself, but I wouldn't put it past him. I'm through being surprised."

Suddenly, an eerie sound was heard at the utterance of Donnie's last words. Eve appeared in the same manner she had earlier.

"Hot damn!" Damien yelped. "Man! Is this what, or who you were trying to warn me about?"

He couldn't keep his knees from knocking with fear.

"Adam! Adam honey, where are you?"

Donnie was now familiar with the phantom figure. This time, no uncontrollable bodily functions occurred.

"Say guys… you haven't seen a big, tall black man wearing animal skin, have you? He's supposed to be here by now."

Then Eve pointedly addressed Donnie and said. *"Donnie, I see you're completely dry for a change."*

The startled man could fill the blood rush to his face from the embarrassment of Eve's callous remark lowering his head quietly answered.

"No, I-I haven't seen Adam."

"Humph… I wonder what's keeping him."

Even though the unexpected shock of Eve's sudden appearance was waning, Donnie focused his attention on the apparition's purpose for visiting his home… yet again.

"And you're here *be-cause?*"

"*Now, I know you know this is not my first visit to your humble abode, so why are you so surprised?*"

"Yes, you're correct." The unintentional host stated. "And you're in my home again *because…?*"

Eve nonchalantly strolled over to the mahogany sofa table, leaving the perplexed host to wonder if she'd heard his question.

Smiling at the familiar surroundings the now familiar apparition lovingly picks up a photo of the home's occupants they had taken during a Caribbean cruise the year before.

"*Hmmm… nice picture.*"

Carefully returning the array of photos on the table turns back to the gentlemen with a devilish look in her eye.

"*I saw you this morning while I was speaking with your wife and her friend…what's her name?*"

"Tonika" Donnie inserted. Eve was slightly amused.

"*So you really do know how to pronounce her given name.*" Eve said with a smile.

She'd long since dismissed her unpleasant opinion of the unbridled character she'd had the unfortunate pleasure of meeting.

"*You know guys, I couldn't help but over hear your conversation a while ago. So what exactly did you mean by asking…did Adam ask God for that woman?*"

"You mean you heard that!" Damien scratched his head in wonderment. "Damn! What don't you hear?"

"*You sound like my husband.*" Eve said. "And *you do know your boy told God, "It was that woman you gave me."* Eve shucked her teeth and turned away again. "*You men are all alike, chips off the old block!*"

Neither of the gentleman cared for her callous statement. Donnie uttered a well-defined expletive.

"Oh, hell no! Now you're wrong on that one Miss Evie!"

Damien decided to interject a bit of biblical fact.

"Hel-lo, news flash!" He exclaimed.

The attention grabber stopped the grand matron in her tracks.

"Woman! Your reputation has preceded you for eons! I don't have to tell you that Adam wasn't the only one that blamed you."

Eve was jolted out of her stupor. The younger of the men now held her attention, even though she disliked what he'd said.

"Go on… I'm waiting to hear." She folded her arms in defiance.

"The Apostle Paul said in1Timothy 2:14 that Adam wasn't the one deceived. He said it was *you*… and that you had become a sinner." Damien felt bolder by the minute.

"Saul-*Paul had his nerves… but what can I say?"* Eve gave Damian the once over. *"And you can talk!"*

She stepped forward until she was toe to toe with her accuser.

"So, what's your excuse for the life you lead? At least I was truthful to my man! And besides he wasn't complete without me."

"If you say so…. It took a moment to recoup from the shock of the apparition's knowledge of his antics.

"Well, I do say so!"

Donnie was amused at the skirmish unfolding before his eyes.

"I guess my man looked so pitiful that our compassionate Father put my baby to sleep and… tada!"

"And I don't suppose your man ever missed that rib!"

Donnie playfully shoved Damien in the ribs with an elbow. Eve chose to ignore it.

"Speaking of my 'short rib,' you sure you haven't seen him?"

"Seen him? I can't even believe I'm seeing you!" Donnie responded.

"Where did you come from anyways? You were already here with my wife, so why the return visit?"

"Yes, I was."

"Why do you people, I mean you ghosts keep popping up in my house? And aren't you supposed to be in Heaven somewhere?"

"Yikes!"

Damian jumped about four feet in the air. The appearance of another unimaginable creature had suddenly manifested out of nowhere.

The man called Adam stood a towering six feet. His chiseled body gleamed like the finest polished black onyx. The shiny onyx head was supported by a neck the size of a young oak.

Piercing eyes encased in sockets set far apart under a protruding brow searched the unfamiliar surroundings. A strong jaw and a narrowed nose with flaring nostrils completed the handsome being.

His physique boasted a flat stomach etched in a six pack, well defined with deep crevices between each muscle. Long, sculptured arms that extended well below mid-thigh hung from broad, muscular shoulders.

Adam sported a hairy animal loin cloth that was connected from front to back by a strong black cord. Massive thighs and bulging calves supported his massive frame.

Admittedly, the two male humans were dwarfed in dimensions in comparison to the sculpted specimen that stood before them.

"*Oh, there you are … don't ever leave me like that again.*" Eve said, cooing in a seductive voice."*You know I almost always get into trouble when you're not with me.*"

"*Now, that you do!*" Adam said in a matter of fact manner. "*You weren't supposed to come here without me!*"

"*Oh, babe, you never could keep up with me, now could you.*"

Eve playfully declared, thrilled to be reunited with her Adam once again.

"*You have got to quit doing that!*" Adam admonished in a thundering voice full of concern.

"*I'm sorry… but I have to tell you, this is not my first visit here.*" Eve said, speaking with false humility, she lowered her head.

"*You mean you've been here before now?*" Adam asked.

Yes, I met Etta Mae, this man's wife." She said pointing to Donnie. "*And her snooty best friend this morning. Can't say I liked them much either, especially the one called To-To, something or other.*"

"To-ni-ka!" Donnie and Damian both chimed in.

"*Okay al-ready! To-ni-ka!*"

"Don't let them get the best of you, babe." Adam tweaked his wife's nose and said softly. *"That's just homo sapiens for you."*

Eve took a hold of Adam's hand and rubbed it against her cheek.

"Did you know they're still mad at me for causing women to go through the pain of childbirth? I hope they know I was the first to suffer! So why are they complaining!"

The two are so engrossed with one another, and so into their conversation that everyone else was temporarily forgotten.

The whole scenario was so absurd and comical that the two hombres shared a much needed laugh.

"Yep," Adam said to the men. *"Like I'm sure these fellows are mad at me for causing them to break a sweat just to make a living. What did the Word say? "If a man doesn't work, he doesn't eat?"*

"Well, I don't sweat when I'm working." Damien said with his voice edged with pride. "I barely push a pencil, or better yet, strike a few keys on a keypad."

"No need to justify why you don't sweat, my brother." Donnie shook his head."I only sweat when I'm on the golf course, myself."

"Well, I am so happy for you two, apparently I didn't mess things up too badly!"

Once again, Adam felt it necessary to reprimand his wife for her disappearing act.

"I really wish you would stay put, you know what happened the last time you went exploring."

"Do I remember... how could I forget? Eve said thoughtfully. She took a few steps back and sauntered over to the window.

"But you do know it was not my fault. My mind wasn't even on..."

Adam walked over to where his wifestood.

"No, it was all my fault; no one put a rock to my head, if that's what you mean."

"Apology accepted." Eve turned to embrace her love."*But I do have to tell you I was pretty upset with you for saying what you said. I even called you a 'wimp' to the ladies today. Sorry!"*

"Apology accepted."

Donnie and Damian looked on in bewilderment. If anyone had told them a situation such as this would come up; they would have bet on the Mega Millions. The chances were just that slim.

Yet, here was the 'first Adam' and first lady in his living room.

"Somebody, please pinch me." Donnie whispered under his breath.

Damian was only too glad to oblige, and reached over to do just that, but was stopped in his tracks with the coldest stare.

They both turned their attention again to the scene being played out in the room.

"But you do know it wasn't until you bit the fruit that everything fell apart!" Eve told Adam.

"Ah, excuse me, 'scuse me." Donnie said, walking over to the pair. "But what are you two doing? In fact, why are you acting like we're not even in the room?"

He was disenchanted with the whole fiasco and continued his tirade.

"Miss Thang' here just waltzes up here in my house like it belongs to her! And you pop up from out of nowhere! There ought to be a law!"

"It is all of you human's fault. Adam retorted. *"You just couldn't leave well enough alone! It's not enough for you to live in this world, but now you're meddling in our world too!"*

"And yes, there is a law and it's written in Deuteronomy 18:11." He went on to say.

"Oh, here we go!" Donnie blurted.

"Didn't God say that man were not to meddle with the spirit world or practice magic or sorcery?"

Adam drove home his point by driving his index finger repeatedly into Donnie's chest.

"But no, as usual, like any other law, you humans find a way to break them all at the drop of a hat."

"You got me pegged wrong dude!"

Donnie backed away from the unwanted contact. He rubbed the invaded area with his hand.

"I don't go anywhere looking for ghosts! It's those geeks on television that's going into haunted houses talking about "speak to me; I know you're in here! Move something!"

And me neither, Damian quickly added. "I don't even watch ghost movies let alone go looking for them."

"Bro'thas, bro'thas!" Adam said.*"I know you two don't. The two of you are… shall we say, quite timid.* The first man laughed a roaring laugh. *"Two big scaredy cats!"*

"I got your scaredy cat."

Damien, defiantly shouted.

"You're a ghost and I'm talking to you, aren't I!"

"Boo!" Adam shouted. *"I'm a ghost and I just spooked you!"*

"Let me out of here… all this crap is crazy!"

Damien brushed past Donnie only to be grabbed by Adam.

"Oh, no you don't Brotha' Man! I came here especially for you."

"What did you say? You came for me! Why, what did I do?"

"I just wanted to tell you that your heavenly Father is not pleased with the way your life is going. In fact, He's not particularly pleased with the way the whole world has gone! Unfortunately, dare I say, due to yours truly."

Both Donnie and Eve watched closely. Adam remained standing as Damien, sat down on the couch. He felt as if the wind had been knocked out of him.

"You got that right! You were weak, man! You should have seen through that wily old serpent." Donnie went over and joined the two.

"It's like I just told my wife, I take full responsibility for my actions." Adam replied. *"I messed up, so you're all going to hell in a hand basket!"*

"Oh, no we're not!" Damian exclaimed. He jumped up from his seat.

"We're not because of what the last Adam did! And those of us that believe on Him are redeemed! Glory be to God!"

There was a look of shock on everyone's face, but they listened intently.

"You're the first Adam, but God's son, Jesus Christ is the last Adam! And He came to save us all, including you two. Hallelujah!"

"Well… aren't you your father's son!" Adam looked at the preaching human with amusement. *"You preach just like him."*

"Look at you! I didn't know you had it in you, brother!" Donnie said, pleasantly surprised at the man's outburst.

"And like Rev. 'D.' here said, if I'm not mistaken, because of Jesus, you and your girl here were even redeemed."

Adam thought perhaps he may have overestimated the situation, and looked thoughtfully at the two men.

"True, true, and I thanked Christ personally when He came to paradise after His death. I'm forever grateful."

He quieted himself by just thinking about the enormous price the Savior paid for human kind. Then he perked up once again.

"You talk about something bright! Oo-wee! There we were on the comfort side of Hades, in Paradise, when all of a sudden, a beam of light brighter than the sun lit up the whole place, even the tormented side."

"What is the tormented side?" Damien asked with concern. "Is hell divided or something with a good and a bad side?"

"It's hard to believe, isn't it?" Adam answered. *"And yes, it was, to answer your question, but not anymore."*

Thinking more on the matter, Adam addressed Damien with a question.

"Wait a minute! You were a 'PK! So, if either of you two would know about hell, it should be you. Your father preached on Luke 16:19-31 one Sunday morning on November 16, 1988. But of course, as usual, you were nodding off!"

"Like I remember every sermon my dad ever preached!" Damien shouted. "Apparently that's where you come in!"

Adam chose not to respond to Damien's outburst, but continued to tell about Jesus' stay in Hades.

"So… for a brief moment in time, hell was lit up! We even got to look in on the darkness over there, and what a horror to behold! Demons squirmed and wiggled and hid their ugly faces. And the tormented people…. O, my Lord! Of course, 'hell' couldn't help but be lit, because wherever He is darkness has to flee! Can I get an Amen?"

"Amen!"

Eve shouted from across the room.

189

"Thanks, babe. I tell you, from what I could see over there, you don't want to go to that place. It is hor-ri-ble! I pity the fool!"

Looking at Damien, then back to Adam, Donnie anxiously proclaimed.

"You see, I told you, I told you! My God will do anything to keep us from that place. He didn't build it for us anyway. It was only meant for Satan and his imps!"

Donnie stood and paced the floor, unable to bridle the excitement he felt at this jubilation.

"Damian, my friend," he said, "have you ever heard of the 'living Bible? Well here it stands, right before our very eyes!"

Damien, who was speechless through the whole spill, stuck his hands between his legs, and hung his head.

"Adam!" Donnie continued. "Just tell me you're not really here!"

Everything was becoming too unbelievable.

"I know what, I'm dreaming and when I wake up, neither one of you will be here, including old Double D."

Donnie said, slapping his own face with a resounding smack.

"Damn!" He said, recoiling from the sting. "That hurt! And all of you are still here!"

The befuddled man took his seat. "That Etta Mae Smith started all this! Now she's nowhere around."

"No, you're not dreaming."

Adam smiled unabashedly over the discomfort their presence caused the two gentlemen.

"And yes, I'm, that is, we really are here."

He drew his woman closer to the inner circle.

"Do you realize that the lies of Satan are behind all the drama that has been going on in your life? Eve said. *"And your father knows exactly what you're up to. You have been led astray."*

"You know my dad!" Damien asked, astonished.

Know him? If it weren't for his request to come and deliver you, we wouldn't be here." Adam assured Damien.

"Deliver me, deliver me from what?"

"All I'm saying is that what you're going through is all due to a deceptive spirit. And the Jezebel spirits along with their friends are behind it all.

They are all controlling, deceitful, as well as, lying spirits that are totally against anything that has been ordained as righteous."

"You're speaking gibberish ... who or what are you talking about?" Damien asked, confused. Donnie looked on.

"Let me break it down for you, brotha.' The spirit of deception and his buddy, that old slimy perverted spirit is hard at work today. "Your world is Sodom and Gomorrah, all over again!" Eve declared.

Damian jumped up, clasped his head in his hands and shouted.

"Spare me please! Now, it's coming from all sides; first Donnie and now you two! A damn spirit! No, two spirits!" He nervously paced the floor.

"I'm talking to two spirits! Somebody, please shoot me."

"Damian!" Eve said, taking him by the hand and holding it in hers.

"Sweetie, you would do well to listen! Even I know that the sin that serpent of a devil brought into the world was to confuse all of mankind about their purpose in life."

"Wait a minute," Donnie said, "I have one question."

"And what is your question?" The power couple asked.

"Why do you two talk like us? Honey this and honey' that! Aren't you supposed to talk bibley-gook, the 'thees' and the 'thous'?"

"Hey, yeah, you're right!" Damien said in agreement. "They sound like they're from the 21st century."

"Ahem!" Eve cleared her throat. *"Allow me, please babe... Guys, you see we travel from century to century, and we take on the persona of the era we land in."*

The befuddled gentlemen shook their heads in recognition.

"Donnie you seem to be doing pretty good." Adam said. *"But, I have to tell you... there is one thing your 'Maker' has against you."*

"And that being?" Donnie sarcastically inquired.

"Thou shall have no other gods before Me!" Sound familiar? Donnie, have you been golfing lately my good man?"

191

Donnie swallowed past a big lump in his throat.

"Y-Yes, I was out there today and on my game. Hey… wait a minute! I go to church, if that's what you're thinking."

The spirit couple looked on in amusement. Donnie continued to justify his actions or lack thereof.

"I just didn't go Sunday, because we had a golf tour-na… ment. He paused before saying softly.

"And besides, you can't stay around Etta Mae Smith, and the Word not rub off on you."

"Do you know what Donnie?" Eve asked.

"What Miss Eve."

"Your wife doesn't actually know where your stance is when it comes to the Father. She does know that you occasionally read your Bible, but you never voice your stand, or add anything when and if you go to Wednesday night Bible study.

May I remind you, of what Jesus said in Revelation 3:1 "I know your deeds; you have a reputation of being alive, but you are dead! Wake up!"

"Well, I dare say, it ain't none of her business!"

Donnie was upset by the fact that he had to face himself, his soul had been laid bare.

It didn't help to realize he'd stood in judgment pretty much a part of the day on Damien's life, but hadn't bothered to examine his own. However, still in defiance, he chose to put on a brave front.

"That's between me and my God. I-I just don't let the old girl know it, but I do listen when she's quoting scriptures." He said in his defense. "Plus the fact with her dragging me to church!"

The spurned man tried to make light of his statement, but the humor wasn't shared by the occupants in the room.

"Just kidding, my wife, in no form or fashion has to drag me to the house of God. Actually, I look forward to going, when I know Pastor Hershel is preaching that is."

He nervously laughed again, and received the same reaction. Finally Eve said.

"Just remember my dear fellow. It is not your wife that you must answer to, but the One who called you 'luke warm.' And, believe me, He will spew you out of His mouth! In other words, the Lord is saying; "Don't play with Me!"

"Oh, you guys are wrong! That scripture wasn't talking about me! Now, you're wrong on that one."

"Case in point!" Damien exclaimed. "Now let's get back to me! The one you appear to know quite a bit about. It seems to me; you ought to be minding your own business."

Well, like I said, Jesus redeemed me, and He can do the same thing for you, my son. Adam addressed Damien directly. *"All you have to do is to "confess with your mouth, and believe in your heart that He is Lord."*

"How're you going to fix your mouth?" Damien shouted. "You see! If you've been watching me as you said, then you would know that I already did just that. And at a young age at that!"

"Did I not say that I had been watching you for a lifetime? How then can you say, I do not know you?" Adam relentlessly quizzed Damien. *"I know when you made your first childlike confession, unfortunately, so does the 'old adversary.' That is why he went after you because of the plan for your life. I came for such a time as this."*

"I don't know why you came here. It's not like you can do anything to save me. Besides, I don't need you to remind me of anything."

The argument between the two was beginning to escalate. Damien didn't care to be reminded of his short comings in the spiritual department and had become resentful of the fact that he was being confronted. Adam, however, meant to deliver on his assignment.

"I have to do, what I have to do."

Now aren't you suddenly the Holy One!"

"No… If I was 'the Holy One' you wouldn't be talking smack; you'd be on your knees repenting."

"Oh, so you're here to put a G.A.G. order on me." Damien said. Puzzled faces stared back at him. "God's Amazing Grace!" He yelled. "Geez!"

"No, I'm not the 'Holy One of Israel' nor do I claim to be."

Laying all humor aside, Adam gave it to Damien with guns blazing.

"I'm merely on assignment. I know what it's like to think you've gotten away with tomfoolery, but God knew, and still knows. Nothing is hidden from Him. He's all seeing and all knowing."

Uh, I believe that's called, 'Omniscient,' He-He's omniscient." Donnie quickly interjected. Only to be silenced by the cold stares.

"And I tell you something else." The 'first human' said. *"It's sad to say that even my first son Cain, who did the unthinkable by murdering his own brother was stupid enough to believe that he could hide the murder from God. But let it be known that everyone's actions have consequences; good or bad.*

My own son allowed his jealousy to turn to anger, then to hate. Even when Abel's blood cried out to God from the ground, to avenge him, your God and my God, had enough love and compassion for the one who took his own brother's life, to place a mark on the murderer's forehead, lest anyone should do him harm."

Eve listened intently, while her husband told of their most heartbreaking moment. All of the tears she had shed over the plight of her two sons had fallen to the cursed earth. Her tears had watered the thorns and the thistles that had sprung up.

"Now bear with me here." Adam droned on. *"The earth then, has become saturated with the blood of your brothers ever since. We're sorry... and we apologize wholeheartedly. That same murderous spirit that caused the death of our beloved son is privy to do the same to your sons and daughters today."*

Eve couldn't take it any longer. She knew her tears had become the forerunner of the many tears mothers would shed through eons to come.

"Look at what is happening every day in your world; blood is constantly spilled, brother killing brother. And all that blood cries out to the Creator each time the earth opens its mouth to receive it.

Mothers are weeping just as I wept that day in the field. Sadly, they will continue to weep."

Adam went over to console his grieving wife. Her small stature was over shadowed as he enveloped her in a warm embrace.

"It's okay, the Lord gave us other sons and daughters to share our love. One by which His only begotten son would bear lineage, so all was not lost. Now dry your tears, we're nearly done here. Okay?"

"Okay... but you know what?" Eve said with a smile.

"What's that dear?"

"When the Father said my seed would crush the head of the serpent, I-I thought He meant it would be our son Cain." She began to sob once again.

"I know you did, I know you did; there, there, now. We eventually got it right."

The captive audience hadn't been able to utter a word. They were so engrossed in the compelling drama being played out. Adam soon returned to the task at hand.

"Your neighborhood gang doesn't realize it, but they're nothing but mere puppets in the hands of the enemy. In the mist of every known gang are representatives of Satan, mainly the 'spirit of coercion.' It compels one to do an act, or to make a choice they hadn't planned to do. It's a 'voice in your head' so to speak. This spirit causes minds to serve evil. Consequently the more they're susceptible to this spirit, the greater the evil they will accomplish.

The gangs will continue to cause death and destruction, because no one can seem to deliver them. At this very moment, your nation is crying over a poor young man's spilled blood, whose life was taken by someone who listened to the voice of the enemy."

"Oh, I feel for all those mothers." Eve interjected. *"Their tears are watering the earth like mine. The whole nation feels the pain.*

It's like Jeremiah 31:15 says; "A voice is heard in Ramah, mourning and great weeping, Rachel weeping for her children and refusing to be comforted, because her children are no more."

She walked away from the men and stood at the window again, sadly looking out.

"I-I know what you're saying is true." Damien said. "And... I heartedly repent of my misdoings. It even grieves me to think about them."

Everyone in the room was deeply touched. A sole tear even cascaded down the unsuspecting host's face.

Adam's preaching had ignited such a flame in the remorseful young man's heart, after suffering deep conviction Damien knelt down and prayed a soul wrenching prayer of repentance.

"O, Lord, I ask you to come into my heart, and renew my mind and my spirit. Heavenly Father, I want the mind of Christ from this day forward. A mind that will love, obey, and do Your 'Will.' Lord, I renounce Satan and all he stands for. I renounce the 'spirit of perversion, and the spirit of false pride' that had me in its grips far too long.

I believe you are the Son of the Living God, and you died for my sins. Lord, your Word says; "though my sins are of crimson," I know your blood can wash them white as snow. Wash me Lord, cleanse me. I want my life to belong solely to you. Lord, I am no longer who man says I am, but I am who you say I am; a son of the Most High God. I surrender my all to you. I have prayed this prayer in the Name of your Son, Jesus the Christ. Amen."

As he knelt there he was enveloped with a sense of peace, love and joy. Damien had never felt so much love. He celebrated by jumping to his feet and shouting aloud.

"Praise the Lord! I have been set free!"

Everyone in the room rejoiced. He ran over to Donnie and began to explain his feelings.

"I truthfully thought everything was acceptable in a no holds barred society, so, I gave into the forbidden desires. And I justified it by telling myself I wasn't alone in my sordid acts.

Everyone is so proud of being the way they are." He said forlornly.

"They all seemed to proudly shout out their hidden secrets with pride."

"Life does have a way of deceiving and bogging you down."

Donnie truly empathized with the young man's plight.

"You're right." Adam said in agreement. *"But, can I tell you the real reason they're all coming out? Their coming out is not of their own choosing, but, it's the 'omniscient one' pulling the covers back. That perverted spirit operated in secrecy far too long; it's now exposed."*

"If that's the case, then why do people gladly admit their preferences?"

"Deceit can no longer hide its ugly head. You read in the Scriptures "everything done in the dark will come to light." If God said it, then it has to come to pass."

"You got that right!" Eve chimed in. *"You can't pull anything over on the 'Big Guy.' I don't know just how long it's going to take you people to realize*

that! Just like me and Adam, we thought we were being slick ...remember babe, when we hid."

"Eve, honey...we've already covered that, but yes, I do remember. Oh, how I remember."

"Sorry babe, I just can't forget. But do carry on, by all means."

"Thank you. and Donnie... to answer your question, the sad thing is, once those perverted spirits have been revealed, a false sense of pride takes over; another trick of the enemy, the 'spirit of pride. And so instead of asking for deliverance, mankind rejoices in their deception.

But the Father does not approve of the vigilante attitude man has acquired. The only thing He wants mankind to do is to love unconditionally. No matter what their takes in life we're all His children."

"Amen to that!" Donnie shouted. "So we don't need to be killing, mutilating or bashing anyone over the head for their life's choices. God does not need our help."

"Here, here!" Damien said.

"Now take my man here." Donnie said. "He grew up in the church!"

"Just where're you going with this?"

"I was just—

"Listen, I don't need you to stand in judgment of me!" Damien angrily shouted. "You don't know what I went through!"

Flashbacks of his life, his boyhood rape, had been particularly running through his head during the whole discussion.

"Oo! Why so much anger?" Donnie tauntingly asked.

"You know nothing is as it seems. How do you know I wasn't turned out at church, huh? Man! The church can't —

"He's right you know." Adam watched the play by play drama and solemnly said.

"Those very spirits can and do live at the church. Your children are not even safe. Now that act alone... Well, the Father said "it is better a 'mill stone' was tied around their necks than to harm his little ones.

All one has to do is read today's headlines, to know no one is exempt. Those powerful spirits, or I should say, principalities, the generals, will take down the most fire preaching, oil slinging, preacher in the pulpit, if they're not careful."

"But, listen gentlemen our time is up here. I believe I've accomplished what I was sent here to do. So I just wanted to leave both of you with this thought.

And that is; God loves you no matter what you do or say. He can't help but love you, because He is 'love.'

And Damien, just to let you know, He heard you when you made your confession in your father's church. I just come to help that confession burn bright in your heart once again.

So that you may experience His Holy Spirit strengthening you, in order that the 'fruit of the spirit,' self-control may over shadow your carnal mind.

Damien, my God, and your God loves you so much that I personally came to speak you into your destiny; to preach His Holy Word.

Now, go with hope in your heart, and peace in your spirit. And begin to declare the victory of your deliverance over every area in your life, where ever you may feel defeated. And I would say, at the moment that would be your marriage."

Adam proceeded to place his hand on the weeping convert's shoulder before offering the last piece of encouragement.

"But take heart my friend; God has already worked it out!"

Then offering his arm, Adam turned to his wife. *"And now my love… shall we?"*

She readily grasped his arm, and they both walked off into oblivion.

"Always remember my noble friends…"Deliverance is always available to you!"

"Wow! Who could say anything after that?" Damien thought. The two of them sat as if frozen in time.

Finally, Damien rose from his seat and offered his hand to Donnie.

"I think I'll head back to the hotel."

The perplexed host accepted the extended hand and stood up.

"Alright, dude."

Donnie was able to say despite the churning in his stomach. The two finished their handshake with a series of hand daps.

"We've been through a lot these past few hours, so I guess that makes us 'bosom buddies' so to speak."

"And I know I have a lot to think on, but I do want to thank you for finally letting me in…Brotha' Man!"

Laughter was the order of the moment as they recalled the earlier fiasco.

"Sorry for the scare."

Grabbing and embracing the once burdened young man, followed with a sound pat on the back, Donnie walks his newly found friend to the door.

Damien turned one last time. He'd wanted to leave a message for Delilah.

"Oh! If, that is to say, when my wife returns, please t-tell her I'm at the Misty Heights Hotel, over on Cedar Street, Room 153."

Before opening the door, he turned and said to his cohort.

"Oh, and tell her … I don't mind waiting." Then he stepped out the door.

Donnie leaned against the closed door for a minute or two. He had much to ponder in his heart regarding his own Christian walk.

"Today has truly been a good, good day!"

CHAPTER
Eighteen

....

Mulling over his thoughts, Josh Gibbons now sat at a stop light on a one-way street with only the smooth humming of the restored vintage Trans Am audible, However, the tranquil moment was abruptly broken by the booming pulsating sound of an approaching car.

Anchored securely in the car's backseat were blaring speakers with decibels that reached ear shattering proportion.

Josh's cherished Trans Am vibrated with every pulsating beat of the obtrusive machine idling alongside it.

Josh quickly looked away after nodding to the car's occupants.

The sound of the revving engine prompted him to look once again.

The driver's thick ringlet curls bounced with every movement of his head as he bobbed to every pounding beat.

"Do you want to race?" The driver mouthed to Josh.

The mean machine rocked to and fro as the driver simultaneously pressed the gas pedal, then the clutch. The supped up vehicle's engine revved even louder.

Not only was the loudness coming from the car, but Josh thought the occupants to be a little unnerving, as well.

He thought he heard a few well-placed expletives coming from the young men, but chose not to acknowledge or accept their challenge. He sped off as soon as the light turned green.

The other car's occupants used this as a challenge and sped up beside him. This time their look was more menacing.

The Trans Am slid easily into a lower gear leaving the challenger in the dust once again. But, true to form, the spurned Iroc-Z easily caught up. Now the two power-horses were neck to neck.

The unsolicited drag race had become frustrating to the Trans Am's driver. Just as he looked over to confront the agitators, he came face-to-face with the barrel of a .357 Magnum.

The handgun was lowered out the window towards him, just as a shot rang out. The culprits then raced off, bowled over with laughter without bothering to see if, or what they'd hit.

Josh felt the blood trickling down his face and tasted the salty liquid in his mouth. He shakily pulled over to the curb to see what damage had been done to him, as well as to his 'cherished chariot.'

Stepping from the vehicle onto wobbly legs, Josh falling backwards allowed the car to support his shaking body. A bystander ran over and inquired of his well-being.

"Are you alright, man?" The concerned gentleman who'd rushed to his aid asked. "You've been hit, you need a doctor. I'll call for one."

"N-No, but thanks, it's not necessary. I'm fine, I don't think I've been shot;just a little shaken is all."

"Well, you do have a nasty cut on your forehead." It's probably from flying glass, but I don't see any other damage. Thank God."

"Here, put this on your forehead."

The gentlemen, dressed in all white offered up his handkerchief to the injured victim.

"This should stem the bleeding;let's get you over to this bench."

"You don't want to do that." Josh said, now focusing fully on the stranger. "I might get... blood all over that white suit of yours."

"Oh, I'm not worried about that." The stranger said. "The important thing is to get you saved."

"Get me what?"

The moment the 'anointed' white cloth touched Josh's head, the flow of blood ceased. He felt as he did before the shooting incident, but was somewhat puzzled.

"Who are you?" He asked the man.

"I'm Master Prophet Eli Cummings." He said, taking the handkerchief from the injured man's face. It had become pristine white once again.

What 'da?" Josh exclaimed. "Am I dreaming or am I dead? Either way, I'm getting away from here."

He began to rise, but his legs felt as if they were made of rubber. He sat quietly, mulling his close call over in his mind.

"You were wondering why those young men would do such a thing, when you hadn't even provoked them. Yet they wanted to kill you."

"As a matter of fact I was… and how d-did…?"

He hadn't bothered to finish his question. Josh had already sensed the encounter was going to be anything but ordinary.

"Well, I hadn't exactly bargained to get my head almost blown off today. If that's what you mean."

"To calm your troubling mind, those young men were only doing what they knew to do.

You were merely a target to fulfill their master's desire. "The enemy only comes but to kill, to steal, and to destroy." I'm sure you've heard that scripture before haven't you?"

"Uh, no, I-I haven't."

The all-knowing prophet knew this, but he'd asked the question to get the young man thinking; to do a little soul searching. The stranger sat quietly, watching closely as the young man sorted out his thoughts.

"I, uh, my wife that is …Tonika, goes to church with our neighbor, but I somehow never found my way to do so."

A crippling pang of remorse shot through his chest, at just the mention of her name.

A muted buzzing sound inside his pants pocket was heard at that moment. Josh pulled out his cellphone and read a text that had come in from his wife.

"*Umph!* That's strange... she wants to talk." Josh said in the air. "Wonder what that's all about."

"You would do well to oblige her." The prophet said."After all, she is the victim here."

Josh sat shaking, as tears began to stream down his cheeks. He had wrestled with the decision all night long as he lay on the couch, while his wife lay sobbing in their bedroom.

What had kept him from going to her?" He wondered. He'd wanted to; to hold, to comfort and to ask for her forgiveness.

Maybe it was pride, or just plain old pigheadedness, or, was it the fear of rejection?

"What had possessed him to throw away his family, to chase behind a Jezebel?" He wondered. His co-worker had warned him, but being hard headed, he hadn't listened.

Karla, as it turned out was only interested In wrecking homes. He had thought he would move in with her; thinking he would be readily welcomed.

Instead, the door had been slammed in his face once she knew his home life was in shambles.

"Oh, no honey! You're no good to me like this!" She had laughed in his face.

"I don't want a full time man. It's too much bother. That's why I make it a practice to only date married men."

Karla had grabbed him by his shirt collar;she had pulled him towards her, and had devilishly whispered.

"I just wanted to see you when *I* wanted to see you, because *I* knew *I* could have you at any given time. And you, my little puppy ... always came running!"

He was hearing her next words even now as if she was saying them at that exact moment.

"Go home to your silly little *wife!* I've had my fill of you!"

Then she had laughed a wicked laugh. Josh swore he saw her eyes turn a bright red.

"How do you feel?" Prophet Cummings asked, bringing the man back in focus.

"I feel as if I've lost everything. I've lost my job, my home, my self-respect, as well as my … soul."

"And what about your wife … where does she come in? Then, there's Ashad, your son, who looked up to you as his father."

"C-Can you make me feel any worse?" Josh asked, cradling his head in his hands. He sat in that position for what seemed like an eternity, before hearing the words.

"You can be forgiven. All you have to do is ask. Just as this hankerchief symbolizes; "though your sins are of crimson, His blood washes them white as snow."

Josh's head jerked up, welcoming the ray of hope he'd just heard.

"*Oh?* Do you think my family will forgive my foolishness, and take me back?" He sat on the edge of his seat.

"It would be so wonderful. Why… I would be the best damn husband …a-and father …"

"No doubt you would Josh Gibbons, but there's someone else you really need to speak with."

"*Who?*" He thought long and hard.

"Oh yes … that's right."

Josh dropped to his knees and bowed his head. He prayed a devout prayer of redemption and forgiveness.

When next he opened his eyes, Josh found himself alone. He had wanted to thank the stranger.

He felt a prompting in his spirit to say "Let the redeemed of the Lord say so!"

"So!" Josh shouted from the depths of his soul.

"I am redeemed!"

CHAPTER
Nineteen

....

E tta Mae observed a lone figure out of the corner of her eye, running along the sidewalk.

"*Look*! That looks like my sister! But what is she doing?"

"Oooh! That is Dee and she's carrying her shoes in her hands!"

Tonika peered around Etta Mae to get a better look. "And she's singing!"

"Well, isn't that something? When I left she was still napping, now here she is skipping down the sidewalk bare feet."

Etta Mae blew her horn and stopped the car in the middle of the street.

"Why if I didn't know any better, that knutt's acting like she's seen Jesus!" Tonika added satirically.

"Yeah, *right!* Now, that would be a first!" Etta Mae rolled down the window and yelled.

"Dee! Hey, Dee!"

The lone figure abruptly stopped, thinking she'd heard her name called. She peered inquiringly at the car's occupants, the evening sun in her eyes made it difficult to see.

"Oh, hey Sissy, guess what!"

She said breathlessly running up to the car.

"You're not going to believe…. Dee said taking a deep swallow.

"Dee! Girl, what are you doing? And why are you out here with no shoes?"

"Sissy… you're not going to believe who I spent the afternoon with!" It was all Delilah could do to try and contain her joy. "Go on guess!"

The muscles in her face ached from all the smiling she'd done. She was filled with so much joy, so much peace and so much happiness.

Dee danced in place, and even twirled around, unable to contain her enthusiasm as she waited for her sister's response.

"Let's just amuse her." Etta Mae said to her passenger.

"Oh … I don't know … Jesus maybe?"

"*How did you know?*" Dee excitedly screamed. "Yes, yes, yes! And I met Him at the Well!"

"*You what…*what well? Girl, this ain't no time to be lying!" Her sister yelled. "Don't play with me like that!"

"*Honest!* Sissy, I'm not lying." Dee said with more conviction than necessary.

"There was this church, o-only it wasn't a church, and the name of it was *Re-Dig the Wells*."

"Girl, get in this car! You must have been in the sun too long!"

Etta Mae pressed the automatic door lock to unlock the back door. Dee slid in, luxuriating in the new car smell and the comfortable leather seats.

Even the unwelcomed presence of Tonika sitting in the front seat, wasn't enough to damper her spirit. Her morning's experience was just too exhilarating.

"Dee, you remember my friend and neighbor, Tonika Gibbons." "Yes… hello."

"Hello Delilah, good to see you again, it's been a while."

"Girl, where are you coming from this time of the day?"

Etta Mae reached back to feel her sister's forehead.

"Ooh! You do feel a tad warm. I sure hope you're not having a heat stroke!"

"No, I'm not having a heat stroke."

Welcoming the cool comfort of the vehicle, Dee allowed her tired frame to fall backwards.

"Why would you think that?"

Etta Mae turned to her friend. "Tonika! What did you just hear my sister say before she got in the car?"

"She said—

"She said she just saw Jesus, didn't she?"

Etta Mae focused her attention in the back seat through the rear view mirror.

"Now does that sound like someone coherent to you, Miss Dee? You;a devout agnostic, saw the Lord!"

"But I did! I did see Him..." She was a bit subdued from her sister's unbelief.

"Well, now Etta Mae, she could have you know." This time, Tonika spoke up. "Look what's been happening to us all day; starting with this morning."

"Oh My God! Toni!" Etta Mae yelled, gulping a deep breath. "You're right!"

Armed with that bit of revelation, the elated believer turned in her seat to address her sister.

"Dee! Delilah Collins! I do believe you! My God can do anything. Anything He wants to do because He is sovereign! Praise the Lord, Hallelujah!"

A warm glow crept from Etta Mae's neck up to her tear-stained face.

"*My God!* My agnostic sister, of all people, has had a glorious Jesus encounter!"

"And that goes to show God can and He will show Himself if you only believe!" Tonika gleefully shouted. "Be-because my God is So-ve-reign!"

The atmosphere inside the car had suddenly become an arena of praise with unbridled tears flowing unashamedly, Tonika and Delilah rocked back and forth calling on the name of Jesus.

Etta Mae closed her eyes and began praying prayer of thanksgiving.

"Father, I don't know how, or what you did to my sister, but I thank you for saving her. Thank you, Jesus! Thank you! Thank you! Thank you. Thank you. Lord! I knew your Spirit was always within her. Father, you've always been with us, through all our ups and downs. And I'm glad you didn't give up on her.

Blessed quietness filled the vehicle. And all eyes were shut. Heads were bowed as the powerful prayer went up.

"Lord, you were there all the time! Again, I just want to say thank you! Daddy! Thank you for honoring my grandmother's dying wish. Praise God, all three of her grand babies now know you as our Lord and our Savior!

Because Lord, …Hallelujah! Your child … my sister … Delilah has come home! Oh, hallelujah! Thank ya' Je-sus!"

Suddenly, the sound of a blaring horn brought the afternoon's praise-a-thorn to an end. Startling the ladies.

The irate driver abruptly swinging his car around them menacingly glaring at the car's occupants.

"Oh no Satan, not today!" Etta Mae commanded wiping tears from her face. "You don't want to mess with me today!"

The car eased forward as soft sobs were heard as she drove on. Nevertheless, the 'Spirit' was still high.

"Sister, I have to tell you about my morning walk when we get home."

"Oh girl, just tell me now. We have time."

"I don't have the strength right now." Dee breathlessly uttered. "But my Lord! Umph, umph, umph!"

"I feel ya' sistah! And He didn't do it without us!" Tonika interjected glancing back at Dee.

"Didn't do what without us?" Dee curiously inquired.

"Oh! It's just that your sister and I had just said to the Lord… we said, "Lord! What ev-er You're doing in this moment, pl-eaz-ze don't do it without us."

"Yes! That's right, we did, didn't we? Etta Mae chimed in. "And just look Dee! He allowed us to share in your deliverance."

About that time Etta Mae's phone rang once again.

"Hello, praise the Lord! Hi, hun. Yes, we're on our way home now. In fact, I'm turning onto the street as we speak."

Etta Mae listened intently as Donnie gave instructions meant for her sister.

"Damien is there, and wants Dee to meet him at the Misty Heights Hotel, you say?"

She glanced in the rear-view mirror to gauge Dee's reaction to what was being said.

"I'll talk to him." Dee said then added.

"Inquiring minds wants to know what room is he in?"

"What room, honey?"

"Room 153 … O-Okay. I'll turn around and take her there now." Etta Mae dared not pass judgment.

"Yes, I agree. Yes, you're right. She does owe him that much."

Tonika couldn't help but overhear the conversation. It would seem as if a change had come over the two.

"Will wonders never cease?"

She said under her breath. Bringing her mind back to her own plight.

Let's face it. Who was she kidding? As happy as she was for the couple. She too, needed mending.

"What about me Lord?" She prayed looking out the window. "Please don't forget about me."

Just at that moment, her cell phone rang. Her husband was on the other end.

"H-hello… Josh…What? Are you there now?" Tonika's heart skipped a beat as she listened intently. "You do? Uh huh. I see."

Reaching for her friend's hand for support, Etta Mae gave the trembling hand a reassuring squeeze.

"I tell you what, I'll be there when you get… In fact, we were almost near home. Only, Etta was about to do a U-turn. She has another errand to run."

Tonika covered the mouthpiece exhaling a deep breath.

"Hey Etta, you know what? It's not that far. I can just walk home from here."

"What gives Tonika?" Etta asks. Giving her friend a puzzling side-glance.

"Oh! I'm sorry Etta." Tonika answers. "This is Josh." She takes a deep breath and then exhales before adding. "And he wants to talk."

"Well… if that's what you want to do, who am I to stop you."

"It is… at least, I believe it is." Tonika said before turning to speak into the phone.

"Okay Josh, I'll meet you at home. O-Okay, see you then. Bye." Gleefully turning once again to her friend unable to contain her excitement the once forsaken wife loudly screams.

Eeeeeeee! He wants to talk!"

"Etta Mae!" Tonika excitedly said. "Girl, let me out! I'll walk home from here!"

Tonika said reaching for the door handle even before the car had come to a complete stop.

"Wait! Let me stop the car first! I swear you two will be the death of me yet!" Etta mockingly said.

Secretly, she was relieved and pleased about the possibility of reconciliation between both couples.

The car rolled to a stop and the exuberant wife jumped out.

"Etta Mae, we have a lot to talk about." Tonika said bending down to pear in the window. "I'll see you tomorrow and I'll feel you in on everything. Okay?"

"Okay. See ya' girlie. Now get home to that hubby of yours!"

"God is a good God!" Tonika declares displaying her best Cheshire cat's grin.

"And if it all works out for you, 'baby girl' then you should be a witness the Lord is a restorer of anything the enemy has stolen!" Etta Mae added.

"Oh, you can best bet I will." Then inadvertently cupping her hands around her mouth shouts into the air. "I'll even shout it from the rooftop!"

About this time, the back seat passenger preparing to occupy the front seat all while sidestepping the still glowing former occupant reaches for the front door handle.

"Bye Delilah!"

Then with a sudden movement, unable to contain her excitement, Tonika grabs and hugs the unsuspecting woman.

"Oh!" Dee shouted. Completely caught off guard. But to her own surprise she found herself returning the warm gesture. And before you knew it both were overcome with a feeling of euphoria.

"Bye…my fr-friend."

Dee was able to say as the embrace was broken. The strange occurrence leaves her in awe.

What just happened? She thought. Why am I feeling so liberated?

Humph! that's strange how something just came over me.

Even Tonika stood shaking under the overwhelming oddity as she began rubbing one hand up and down the sleeve of the other.

Oh! She felt it too. Dee surmised. Dee watched deep in thought.

And to think… it only took two little words and a hug to deliver me from a jealous spirit.

Where did that jealous spirit of mine come from anyways? She thought. There certainly was no need for it.

When I last visited my sister, this woman had shown me nothing but kindness. Heck! There's no rhyme or reason for me to have disliked her in the first place. Father, forgive me."

Then, on impulse, once again Tonika finds herself enveloped in a final hug one last time.

Upon breaking the embrace Dee remarked to her friend; "To everything there is a season…"

To which Tonika chose to complete with the verses befitting their circumstance.

"A time to break down, and a time to build up; a time to weep, and a time to laugh…"

"My friend…" Dee says. "It's our season."

Giving her newly found 'spirit sister' a slight kiss on the cheek, Tonika waves goodbye as she walks away.

Meanwhile, inside the vehicle, Etta Mae is witnessing the unbelievable breakthrough taking place. And is unable to curb the flowing tears running down her cheeks.

"Praise God! Praise God!"

As Dee turns to open the car door, she cast her eyes upward towards the sky.

On this day, the brilliance of the bright blue sky filled with white fluffy clouds appearing to have congregated out of nowhere, catches the highly strung observer off guard.

Somehow, she couldn't shake the thought of perhaps heaven was smiling down on her.

All to which, becoming inundated with loving memories of her dearly departed mother and father was unavoidable.

So much so, while intently staring at the clouds the scripture Grams, her devoted grandmother used to comfort she and her sisters easily coming to mine.

"Therefore, since we're surrounded by such a great cloud of witnesses..."

Instantaneously, Dee's hands are raised towards heaven as a radiant smile crosses her face.

Even the sound of the driver's side door opening and her concerned sister stepping out was enough to deflect her intent gaze.

"What're you—

Etta Mae began, questioningly following her sister's gaze.

"Mom and Dad are pleased you know." Dee said without lowering her gaze.

"What! What brought that on?" The bewildered older sister asked. "Are you alright?"

But before Dee could answer, Etta Mae's eyes lit up with a divine revelation.

"Ooh! It's the clouds, isn't it?" she said in a sudden awareness. "You're thinking about Gram aren't you?"

"Yes!!" Dee shouted through the beginning tears. "How did you know?"

"Oh, it's just that her uplifting words comforted us so, after Mom and Dad's death. That's how. And after today's happenings nothing surprises me."

The flood of memories brought on by the melancholy moment resulted in a crying fest among the two.

"And you know, Dee, just looking at those clouds, "Etta Mae began, "Gram's words are as comforting today as they were then.

Though our parents were gone, Gram gave our little minds hope when she said to us, "Little ladies, mom and dad are in Heaven now. But if you live right, you'll see them again."

"Then 'little sister' you remember, asked her, "How?""

"Well…Gram had answered. Because "we who are still alive will be caught up together with them in the clouds to meet the Lord in the air. Besides, they're watching over you even now from the clouds.""

"Yeah, and I remember saying; "Oh! Then I can also bring my dollie with me when we go!" Dee had asked her granny in innocent naivety.

Uncontrollable laughter erupted between the two sisters behind the absurdity of it all.

"And you remember our little sister saying to you; "No silly! She can't go! She'll fall through the clouds!" Etta Mae added still laughing hysterically.

"Silly goose." Dee laughingly added. "And just look at our little sister now. Basically, a walking, talking book of knowledge."

"That she is…that she is."

Etta said in agreement before lifting her arm to check the time.

"O-ooh! G-irrl, we really have to get going. You do have a hot date remember."

"Oh! Oh yeah! That's right I do. Don't I?"

Simultaneously reaching for their individual doorhandles, Dee hesitates.

"You know what Sis? Today has really been an eye opener for me."

"Chile…you ain't even lied! Humph!" Etta Mae said vigorously shaking her head in agreement.

"And you know what Sister!" Dee gleefully asks.

"What?"

"You'll be pleased to hear…" Deliberately drawing it out Dee continues.

"I no longer share in that agnostic viewpoint after today. Especially, since meeting the 'man in white.'"

"Oh, you mean since you met Jesus." Etta knowingly deduced. "And you what 'baby girl'." She went on to add.

"I can truthfully tell you, now that you are a bona fide believer, and is now what we call a 'witness', if you will," she said emphasizing quotation symbols with her fingers, "one day you will see Mom, Dad, and Grams in the clouds."

They're now once again seated and buckled into their seats before Etta Mae thinks to add.

"Oh! By the way. That is, of course, if you "keep your hand on the plow and hold on.""

Dee shivers hearing the life-inspiring words. Giving her beloved sister a reassuring pat on the leg, Etta Mae starts the engine and eases into traffic.

Reading Group

Discussion Questions:

1. *Finding a Happy Medium* is a sequel to the critically acclaimed Cloudy Witness/Blessedly Assured. Both works are inspirational fiction. Both are steeped in biblical history and scripture. How did the scriptural (witnesses) characters set the foundation for Janette Jones' novels?

2. Etta Mae Smith was thought of as being a 'Bible-thumper.' (Someone perceived as aggressively imposing their Christian values and knowledge upon others). How did Tonika benefit from her friend's knowledge of scripture; or did she?

3. How would you characterize or describe Tonika? Would you consider her as being weak, naive or strong?

4. Supernaturalism invading naturalism is the core behind this book. Did the author peek your imagination strong enough for the phenomena to be believed?

5. What did you enjoy most about either or both aspects of the story?

6. Why do you suppose Etta Mae Smith was singled out as the 'go to person' by the biblical spirits? Do you believe all the others were affected by their association with Etta Mae? If so; then please explain.

7. What were your thoughts on Damien and Delilah's relationship? Did you believe Damien's conversion? Was Josh's conversion believable?

8. Mediums and psychics are common place today. The Bible speaks on such practices. But Stephanie's experience was so unlike that of her cohorts. How are psychics, mediums, or Empaths effecting people's lives today?

9. Angels are ministering spirits. Some have entertained angels without knowing it. What was your take on the 'Angel Breakthrough?' How was he able to assist in the Whitman's marriage?

10. One would doubt Mary and Martha had attitudes in Jesus' delay in coming to their brother's aid. In this inspirational fiction their true feelings were made known in a boisterous manner. What was your take on the embellished attitudes portrayed by the two women? In whose disposition were you most compatible?

Meet Janette

As a native North Carolinian, Janette began writing at an early age; writing many poems, essays and short stories through the years. Under the auspice of her church Janette adapted, wrote, produced as well as directed performances such as the 'Passion of the Christ,' and the *'Twelve Steps to the Cross'* done totally in 'mime.'

She later branched out into the Omaha community. In 2002 Janette's first stage production was launched. Whereby, she wrote, produced and directed *Sistah Girl*. The production received rave reviews; ending after a successful run. Then In 2005 *Sistah Girl Revisited* manifested. *Sistah Girl Now & Again,* done in 2008 was presented as a tribute to a deceased beloved cast member.

Cloudy Witness/Blessedly Assured published in 2012 was Janette's first attempt in becoming a published author. The book is an inspirational work of fiction derived from a combination of both *Sistah-Girl* and a 'night vision' she experienced in which cloud-like angelic beings accompanied a likewise figure seated on a throne. This literary work is solely based on the scripture of Hebrew 12:1 "Therefore, since we are encompassed about by such a great cloud of witnesses..."

Finding a Happy Medium, is the sequel to Janette's first novel. It is greatly anticipated by her readers as it picks up where *Cloudy Witness* left off.

Janette's acting debut came to fruition as a featured personality in the Omowale Akintunde's Emmy Award winning 2009 documentary; *'An Inaugural Ride to Freedom: The Legacy of a People, a Movement, and a Mission'*. The documentary depicted a cross country bus trip by college students and members of the Omaha community to the inauguration of President Barak Obama.

The following year in 2010 Janette was cast as Evelyn in Omawale's film *'Wigger.'* Whereby she was honored to work alongside such acting greats as the late Meshach Taylor (Designing Women), and Anna Maria Horsford (Amen, Wayan Brothers and Reed Between the Lines).

On September 14, 2016, Janette became a licensed minister and serves as a local elder in the Allen Chapel African Methodist Episcopal Church in Omaha, Nebraska.

I Liked It!!
"This is a book on a subject that you don't hear about every day. I think more writers should write like this!"
Stacy C.

Truly a blessing - a definite MUST read!

"This book spoke to me! It was very encouraging and uplifting but at the same time entertaining. This book will give you a greater understanding of just how good God is! My only complaint is that I wish it was longer!"

lizberry.

Highly recommend this book. Wonderful writing!

"I started this book and was pulled into every page. This book makes you laugh and it makes your spirit grow. It's also a very good way to read about the Bible with different characters. I loved it and highly recommend this book. I did some research and this is the author's first book and she nailed it. Thank you for the wonderful book."
NCniece.

Available on line
Amazon
And all on line book retailers!

Facebook.cloudywitness.com

Sistah' Girl Takes Center Stage
By Dana Taylor

The third production of local playwright Janette Jones' "Sistah' Girl" was given last Sunday at the Joslyn Art Museum's "Witherspoon Concert Hall" to an enthralled crowd. Show time was at 6:00 P.M. The musical is based on conversations between two friends, Etta Mae Smith, a devout "Bible thumper" full of stories and her newly saved apprentice, Tonika Gibson. The talk is "about any and everything". The subject matters revolve around the role of women in the Bible, how they saw things, what things happened to them, and what things they caused to happen. In addition, Mrs. Jones wanted to adapt the portrayal of these events to language used today, which offered a unique *perspective*. Sistah' Girl was written one year ago.

Producer, writer, and director Janette Jones (l) and Mistress of Ceremonies Millicent Long (r)

According to Mrs. Jones. "The inspiration to write this production, Jan felt, was prompted by the "Holy Spirit" after she thoroughly read the Old and New Testaments". Mrs. Jones said when she began writing the play, "it just flowed". She finished writing the play in one week. The first two productions were performed at the College of Saint Mary's Bridget St. Bridget Theater in June of this year. Since those first productions, two characters have been added to lengthen the performance.

Martha (Tre' Love) l and Mary (Rachel Sanders) during a musical scene.

The additional characters, Martha and Mary of Bethany played by Tre' Love and Rachel Sanders, respectively, have been well received. Those in the audience were treated to a spiritual message that teaches and entertains. In addition, the musical is loaded with talented performers with extraordinary voices and abilities. Mrs. Jones is hoping to take her show on the road in the future, but that will be dependent upon her ability to gain sponsors.

l to r, ⊠Ettae May (Mona Lisa King-Ward, Tonika (Tammy Freeman), and Stephanie (Tia Robinson) talking at the bus stop.

Cloudy Witness: Blessed Assured is a uniquely witty entertaining novel with twists that send the reader on a real adventure saturated with God's word. Janette Jones creatively stretches the imagination with character "appearances" throughout the book. I love how the book puts on display the African American marriage/ love relationship with the funny dialogue/ banter between Etta Mae and her husband Donnie. (He reminds me of my Daddy.) Etta Mae's everyday ministry with her neighbor Tonika, her sister Delilah and her husband Damien, along with gossiping frenemies shows that ministry opportunities are around us daily. The writing is superb and biblical lessons are on full display. A must read; great for a book club.

Cheryl Williams
1st Lady Risen Son Baptist Church

Girl! Chapter 15 just brought me to tears! And I'm sitting in the break room at work! Something about Dee finding her lost faith in the arms of her redeemer, those tears just came out flowing strong!
    Ha-ha. I'm enjoying it so far!
    Thank you for writing it!
Tanya S., Omaha, NE

Author/Playwright Janette Jones has done it again!

Finding a Happy Medium
the Sequel is also now available!

It's Super Natural!

Follow us on:
Authorjanettejones.com
www.jusian.com
Facebook: Cloudy Witness
https://www.pinterest.com
https://janjones.tumblr.com/

BOOK SUMMARY

....

"Therefore, since we are surrounded by such
a great cloud of witnesses…"

Hebrews 12:1a NIV

Riveting Revelations!

*The extent of emotions embedded in this awe-inspiring work of Christian
fiction are endless!*

Therefore, a proverbial warning must be hereby issue." **Beware! It's a real
page turner!"**

*This book is chalked full of supernatural encounters wreaking havoc between
the 'then' and 'now.' In this suspenseful collaboration of scripture and fiction,
earth's atmosphere will supernaturally become the short-term reality for a select
few witnesses that supposedly make up that 'formidable cloud. Whose only goal
is personally telling their story. Experience the emotions, feelings, and desires
of the likes of Eve, Jezebel, Mrs. Potiphar!*

*For next door neighbors, the Smiths, the Gibbons, the Whitmans, and joint
friend, Stephanie, a paranormal invasion of the 'biblical-kind' is definitely
something to behold!*

Milton Keynes UK
Ingram Content Group UK Ltd.
UKHW040736200324
439740UK00003B/47